Garmisch-Partenkirchen

You've Seen the Castles... Now What?

By Susan C. Steinke

DEDICATION

To Rick

You asked me to travel the world with you.

I'm so glad I said yes!

Life with you has been an adventure!

Contents

An idyllic Bavarian town nestled at the foot of the Alps…

This explains why my family has enjoyed living in Garmisch-Partenkirchen for more than ten years.

My hope is to **inspire** you to get off the tourist path and

discover the **hidden gems** of Garmisch…

the ones only locals know about!

After visiting Bavaria's famous castles, what else should you see or do in this gorgeous tourist destination?

This book is written with each season in mind, so that no matter when you visit, you will always have plenty of unique and traditional suggestions to choose from.

I wish you a wonderful experience in Garmisch-Partenkirchen and the surrounding areas!

WINTER

1.

WINTER

Highlights:

- Christmas Markets -*Weihnachtsmärkte*
- Krampus Run -*Krampuslauf*
- New Year's Ski Jump - Neujahrsskispringen
- Horn Sled Racing -*Hornschlittenrennen*
- Audi FIS Ski World Cup – *Audi FIS Ski-Weltcup*
- Deer feeding -*Wildfütterung*
- Barrel Makers' Dance -*Schäfflertanz*
- French Market -*Le Marché Francais*
- Carnival -*Fasching*

CHRISTMAS MARKETS - *WEIHNACHTSMÄRKTE*
November - December

There is no more perfect image of Bavaria than a Christmas market: small wooden stalls lined up next to one another, trimmed with lush pine branches with white lights, the fragrance of *Glühwein* (mulled wine) in the crisp winter air, and a dusting of fresh white snow. The *Christkindlmarkt* is a tradition that takes place all over Germany as early as November through Christmas Eve.

Add a "*schluss*" to your *Glühwein* or hot cocoa! This additional shot of amaretto in your drink will keep you warm, while adding a nice nutty flavor.

Traditionally, these markets open the first Sunday of Advent. In larger cities, such as Munich and Nuremberg, Christmas markets are open every day during the Advent season. The smaller villages feature more unique markets and may only be open for one weekend. These Christmas markets are the perfect place to find locally handcrafted gifts.

Garmisch-Partenkirchen

Garmisch has a small, very charming market at the Richard Strauss Platz, which is open daily. Everything from craft stalls and musical entertainment to roasted chestnuts, *crêpes*, *raclette*, and *Glühwein* can be found here.

Partenkirchen has its own Christmas market, as well, but it is usually only open on selected weekends.

Oberammergau

Oberammergau's market features stalls from local clubs and organizations. Everything is homemade and a large percentage of sales go to charity. This Christmas market is open for only one weekend. Information is available at the tourist office or online. http://www.ammergauer-alpen.de/Media/Veranstaltungen/Christkindlmarkt-Oberammergau-Der-Markt-mit-Herz

Munich

Munich has more than twenty markets throughout the city, including one (complete with an ice-skating rink) at the airport! The most popular market can be found in the town center at the *Marienplatz*, but only a few blocks away in the *Hofgarten*, you will find a medieval-themed market. With a small entrance fee, the Tollwood Christmas Market on the *Theresienwiese* features international theater productions and over 200 tents with crafts and food items. The highlight here is the New Year's Eve party complete with a midnight waltz.

Augsburg

Dating back more than 500 years, this is Germany's oldest *Christkindlmarkt*. The Angel performances are what make this market unique. With the stunning backdrop of a 16th-century city hall,

the last bell will sound in the Perlach Tower and the city hall goes dark. One by one, the windows of the city hall light up, each illuminating an angel as the choir begins to sing. It is spectacular! Angels perform each Friday, Saturday, and Sunday at 18:00. On December 23rd, the program changes slightly, taking place at 19:00.

You can reach Augsburg easily by car (one hour), train (two hours), or the new Meinfernbus (three and a half hours), a comfortable passenger bus that runs between Garmisch-Partenkirchen and several other cities as well as the Munich airport.

KRAMPUS RUN - *KRAMPUSLAUF*
December

In the midst of the Munich's festive Christmas market, evil-looking beasts suddenly appear in the *Marienplatz* to wreak havoc and punish bad people. This 500-year old tradition celebrates Krampus, the companion of Saint Nicholas. While Saint Nicholas rewards good children with gifts, Krampus puts fear into wicked people and bad children.

The *Sparifankerl Pass* (Bavarian dialect for "devil-group") has reintroduced this Alpine tradition. Each member of the group is responsible for their own complex and elaborate costumes. A master carver is commissioned a year in advance to create hand crafted masks from lime, stone pine, or alder wood. Shaggy fur, claws, horns, and loud bells complete this terrifying look. A costume can range from €1,800-2,500.

With over twenty-five appearances in Bavaria, Austria, and northern Italy, you do not want to miss this. You can check dates on the group's webpage: http://www.muenchen.de/rathaus/home_en/Tourist-Office/Events/Christmas/Erlebnis_e.

NEW YEAR'S SKI JUMP- *NEUJAHRSSKISPRINGEN*
January

It all started about sixty years ago, when ski jumping friends from Innsbruck and Partenkirchen had the idea to start their own tournament. Today, as part of the Four Hills Tournament (*Vierschanzentournee*), Garmisch-Partenkirchen has the honor to be the second event in the series. The *Vierschanzentournee* officially opens in Oberstdorf, followed by Garmisch-Partenkirchen, Innsbruck and finishing in Bischofshofen. Originally, the competitors would jump over a wooden platform off the Kochelberg, which is now nothing more than an overgrown area. As you face the ski jump, this area is to the right of the chair lift.

Today, sixty-two meters above ground, competitors begin their descent. With a 74% grade, it is no surprise that an athlete's blood pressure goes from 80 up to 190 when they become airborne. This architectural structure replaced the previous ski jump, "The Old Lady," in April 2007, with construction taking a mere eight months.

Each year, the New Year's annual ski jumping competition is held here at the Olympic Stadium. Originally built for the 1936 Winter Olympics, this stadium could accommodate up to 130,000 spectators.

How is ski-jumping scored?

Five judges give points for distance and style and/or technique. Each judge is allowed twenty points per participant; the lowest and highest scores are discarded.

- Distance: The "K-point," or critical point, is a determined line where the steepest part of the hill transitions to the flat ground. Each participant earns sixty points for landing on this line. Points are deducted if they land too short or added if they land past the K-point. In Garmisch, the K-point is currently 125 meters.
- Style and Technique: These are points for style execution, such as: ski stability and straightness, arm position, style, landing, and body position.
- Wind conditions are calculated for each participant at the time of the jump.

Ticket reservations are recommended and available in advance at the GAP-Ticket, Richard-Strauß-Platz (+49 8821 730 1995) or online at www.gapa.de.

Tours of the ski jump are also available by contacting the tourist information office. Cost: Adults €10, Children €8. +49 8821 180 700.

HORN SLED RACING - *HORNSCHLITTENRENNEN*
6 January

Traditionally, farmers would transport hay from the Alpine meadows to the
valley using large wooden sleighs, with
runners up to three meters in length. Forty
years later, local people continue the
tradition in an annual competition with
teams of four participants racing down a 1.2-
kilometer path, lined by tall wooden walls
and reaching speeds up to 100 kilometers per
hour. It is exciting, with plenty of crashes,

daring moves, and silly fun. You just can't make this stuff up! It is definitely
worth watching.

There is a small admission price.

As with any German event, *Bratwurst* and beer stands are plentiful.
The Bratwurst is a deliciously moist German sausage made from
eal, pork or beef, served fresh off the grill in a baguette bun. There is
o better spectator snack!

Location: Olympic Ski Stadium - follow the pedestrian road toward the
Partnachklamm (10-15 minute walk).

AUDI FIS SKI WORLD CUP – *AUDI FIS SKI-WELTCUP*
January

Garmisch is part of this exciting racing circuit and
home to the world class Kandahar ski slope. Break
away from your cozy living room and see the action
first hand at the base of the Kreuzeck and
Alpspitzbahn lifts. Racing weekends for men and
women are typically one week apart, with the men's
races at the end of January. Women's races are

usually the first weekend of February.

Tickets can be purchased in advance at the Gap-Ticket, Richard-Strauss-Platz, Phone +49 8821 7301995 in Garmisch-Partenkirchen or online http://www.fis-ski.com/alpine-skiing/index.html.

A great way to see the athletes up close without the crowds is to observe the teams practicing in the mornings a few days before the big race!
At the bottom of the Kandahar run, near the Kreuzeck lift, you can walk right up to the finish lines and watch your favorite athletes do their practice runs. Practice run times are posted here: http://www.fis-ski.com/alpine-skiing/index.html. Your chances of getting a selfie and autograph are pretty good!

DEER FEEDING - *WILDFÜTTERUNG*
January

Only a short walk from the Berggasthof Almhütte, on the Kramerplateau, you can witness the majestic red deer being fed. The local gamekeeper, Willie Erhardt, will tell you all about these animals and everything you need to know about how local forest rangers help them make it through the long winters.

Surrounded by nature, with snow on the ground, this is quite an amazing sight, especially when Mr. Erhardt "calls" the deer. Over fifty deer just seem to appear out of the forests.

Reservations are mandatory.

Garmisch: Contact information and feeding times are available at: http://www.gapa.de/Garmisch-Partenkirchen_Events-Dates_News?story=1590&watchlist=true.

Open December 26 - late February, Thursday - Sunday at 16:00.

Cost: Adults €3, Children up to 6 years, €1.

Location: Park at Berggasthof Almhütte, Maximilianshöhe 15, 82467 Garmisch-Partenkirchen.

Oberammergau: Contact information and feeding times are available at: http://www.ammergauer-alpen.de/ettal/Naturlandschaft-Ettal/Wildtierfuetterung-Graswang

Open: December 27 - March 15, Friday - Sunday at 16:00. February - March, at 17:00.

Cost: Adults €3, Children up to 6 years, €1.

Location: Park at Schattenwald, Ettal. Paid parking is available.

BARREL MAKERS' DANCE - *SCHÄFFLERTANZ*
Every seven years

In the 16th century, when Europe was enduring the plague, it is said that barrel makers were the first to dance in the streets in order to spread joy and hope amongst the townspeople. The Schäfflertanz has been a part of Partenkirchen history since 1834. This impressive celebration is performed every seven years, from the New Year until Ash Wednesday, with the next celebration in 2019. Twenty-five participants, wearing the traditional barrel makers' costume of bright red jackets, green hats (complete with a large white plume), and black pants with white stockings perform impressive dances with boxwood branches shaped into an arch above their heads.

With the barrel rings wrapped in greenery, a series of nine dances are performed:

- Invasion: The greeting and formation of the circle.
- Snake: Representing the dragon that spreads poisonous plague breath upon the city.
- Arbor: A tight formation of four, symbolizing the confinement people felt during the plague.
- Cross: A symbol of faith and hope.
- Crown: A symbol of the ruling house under the Wittlesbach family and Duke Wilhelm IV.
- Four circles: Five dancers in four small groups representing the wheels turning; things are working again.
- Iridescence: Each dancer with his own boxwood branch symbolizing

- that each has their own life back; in this dance, they greet each other.
- Tire swing: One dancer will stand upon a barrel and intricately swing two rings above his head.
- Departure: The final departure.

If this traditional costume sounds familiar, you may have recognized it from Munich's *Glockenspiel*, the clock tower, in the center of Munich's Marienplatz. At 11:00 and 12:00 daily, the clock chimes and the small figures come to life, performing a miniature version of the *Schäfflertanz*. From March to October, this also occurs at 17:00 daily. To find out where and when the *Schäfflertänzer* will be performing in Munich, you can refer to the following website: http://www.schaefflertanz.com. At the time of this publication, the next *Schäfflertänz* will be in 2019.

FRENCH MARKET - *LE MARCHÉ FRANCAIS*
February

For five days, the Richard Strauss Platz is transformed into a quaint French market. With over twelve stands featuring French delicacies such as wines, homemade cheeses, sausages, baguettes, croissants and macarons, you may find it hard to resist the choices! It is a perfect spot to come and enjoy lunch or dinner. Since dates for this market fluctuate each year, it is best to check the website for current dates: http://www.le-marche-francais.de/termine/.

The best I can tell you is that this market comes to Garmisch anywhere from late January to mid-February.

CARNIVAL - *FASCHING*
January-February

Men are disguised head to toe by hand-carved wooden masks (*Maschkera*), Trachten (traditional clothing) and gloves. They are typically disguised as women and carefully covered so that no one will recognize them. Even their speech is more like grunting for fear that a friend or neighbor would recognize them. Carnival, known as *Fasching* in southern Germany, officially begins on 11 November at 11:11. However, most celebrations start on 6 January, the Feast of the Epiphany. The word *Fasching* dates back to the 13th century and comes from the word *Fastenschank*: the last serving of alcohol before Lent. While the word *Fastnacht* comes from the word *fasen*: to be silly, foolish. The festivities come to an end on Shrove Tuesday. The following day, Ash Wednesday, is the beginning of the Lenten period.

The highlights of the Fasching period are special foods, parades, and sudden surprise appearances of small groups of *Fasching* revelers who mischievously entertain restaurant guests. The *Bäckerei* (bakery) windows are filled with colorful *Krapfen*, delicious cream-filled doughnuts.

In the week prior to Ash Wednesday, each day has a specific theme:

- Thursday before Ash Wednesday: Fat Thursday, *Schmotziger Donnerstag*
  Parades and the "handing over the city keys" will take place, giving power to the fools. In Garmisch-Partenkirchen this is also *Weiberfastnacht*, the night when the women have power. On this day, the women—symbolically—cut off the men's ties!
- Friday before Ash Wednesday: Sooty Friday, *Rußiger Freitag*.
  On this day, it is customary to smear soot on children's faces.
- Monday before Ash Wednesday: Rose Monday, *Rosenmontag*.
  This day is celebrated with a parade.
- Shrove Tuesday, *Fastnacht*. Traditionally, this is the last big party before Lent.
  Many of the restaurants will have festivities, but you do have to reserve your table in advance. Be advised you should wear a costume of some sort; otherwise you will be subject to mischief! I can recommend the following restaurants:

Gasthof zur Schranne, Griesstraße 4, Garmisch-Partenkirchen +49 8821 9098030.

Gasthof Schatten, Sonnenbergstraße 10-12, Garmisch-Partenkirchen +49 8821 9430890.

Gasthof zur Rassen, Ludwigstraße 45, Garmisch-Partenkirchen +49 8821 2089.

Werdenfelser Hof, Ludwigstraße 58, Garmisch-Partenkirchen +49 8821 3621.

"Hut to Hut" – Fasching on the Mountains

If you are feeling more adventurous, then I propose the traditional "Hut to Hut" skiing/sledding. The objective is quite simple; you begin at the top of the Alpspitze and continue to the *Drehmöser 9 Hütte* (Hausberg). From the top of the Alpspitze, you will stop at each hut, enjoying the festivities along the way: Alpspitze bar, *Hochalm*, *Kreuzeckalm*, and *Bayernhaus*. Did I mention that this is all in the evening after the lifts close? Yes, you start the night off by catching the last gondola at the Alpspitze at 16:00 (even if advertised for 16:30,  don't risk it.) You should definitely wear a costume and bring a bright headlamp. There are no illuminated ski trails or gondola services available. Skiing and sledding are at your own risk.

I recommend getting a reservation or squeezing into either the *Hochalmhütte* (+49 8821 2907) or the *Kreuzalm* (+49 8821 3045) near the Kreuzeck gondola.

Because the *Drehmöser 9* is now managed by the Zugspitze, it is usually reserved for private events, so don't expect it to be open.

Ash Wednesday
1st day of Lent

As a religious holiday, there are many church processions celebrating the start of the Forty-Day-Lenten season. It is not an official holiday, but a day of reflection, penance, and the start to anticipation of Easter. Since meat and fatty foods are often given up during the observance of Lent, don't be surprised to see that the bakery windows are suddenly void of those delicious *Krapfen*. Be sure to enjoy joy them while you can!

2

SKIING

Conquering the Alps

Ski season begins in mid-December for the Garmisch-Partenkirchen area. For up-to-date weather and snow conditions, I recommend www.bergfex.com. Although the ski areas on the glaciers in Austria are open earlier in the season, be advised that you won't always be able to ski to the valley, so check before you go.

Garmisch Classic Area: The Hausberg, Kreuzeck and Alpspitzbahn offer more than 60 kilometers of skiing combined. You can test your skills on the internationally famous world cup run, the Kandahar, with a vertical drop of 900 meters (2,952 ft.) The downhill record is less than two minutes! Lyndsey Vonn celebrated her 76th World Cup victory with a time of 1:40:80 in 2016.

My favorite run is the Osterfelder run, which starts from the top of the

Alpspitzbahn. As you begin your descent, you must build up speed mid-way so that you can glide between two massive rock formations, and continue toward the Kreuzeck with a fun detour (when open) down the Bernadine run.

Honestly, I have never had a bad meal on the mountain, but I do have three recommendations:

Hochalmhütte (1705m). This hut is pure rustic mountain décor, right down to the deer antler table centerpieces! Known for their game specialties, such as deer or *Gams*, you will not be disappointed with the quality of food. Arrive from Alpspitzbahn and Hochbahn.

Kreuzalm (1600m). Recently renovated, this beautiful Tyrolean-style restaurant is perfect for large groups and a warm and open atmosphere. Try their *Knödel* specialties (dumplings) and *Kaiserschmarrn*! Reach this from the Kreuzeckbahn.

Bayernhaus (1280m). With stunning views, this is the perfect place to escape the crowds. Ask for Oma's *Apfelkuchen,* a delicious homemade apple cake with a crumble top. It is rarely featured on their menu. Arrive from Hausberg.

Zugspitze: When you ski Germany's highest mountain, it will reward you with 360° views and five months of great snow. This ski area is easily accessible with the Zugspitzbahn train or the gondola from the Eibsee parking area. In April 2017, a newer and faster gondola will transport 120 persons up to the summit in no time.

Make sure to walk up the next flight of steps to the summit where you can straddle the border between Austria and Germany. Each terrace is connected by a narrow walkway, which was originally the border control crossing. The Golden Cross on the German terrace is a replica;

The Ski Formula - Chances are that you will be skiing during high season. When it comes to lift lines and getting a table at your favorite mountain hut, my friend, Jim Turro, has developed this no-fail formula. We have tested it, and it works! **8:30-9:00** start your ski day early **10:30-11:00** take your first break; this will give you energy to keep going. **13:00** Lunch (With the majority of skiers taking their lunch at noon, you will enjoy shorter lift lines and plenty of tables when they return to the mountain). **14:30-15:00** enjoy your last runs for the day and depart before the mass exodus.

the original can be seen at the Werdenfels Museum, located at Ludwigstrasse 47 in Garmisch-Partenkirchen.

Cross Country Skiing

With a decent winter and sufficient snowfall, this alpine valley offers groomed **tracks for both classic and skating styles,** free of charge.

In **Garmisch**, there are more than 27 kilometers of long, flat, groomed trails from the Hausberg parking area all the way to Grainau. Grainau offers 16 kilometers of groomed trails, including an illuminated circuit for evening enthusiasts.

You will find these marked trails in the flat meadow area between the Zugspitzbahn tracks and St. Martinstraße.

Oberammergau, only 30 minutes away, is home to the King Ludwig Race. With over 160 kilometers of prepared trails in the Ammergau Alps, the higher altitude helps ensure that one can ski from December until March. Both classic and skating style trails are prepared, and are great for beginners. All the trails are connected, so you can ski from Ettal to Linderhof or Ettal to Oberammergau. It is up to you!

There is an excellent and very detailed *Loipenplan* available for download at: http://www.ammergauer-alpen.de/en/Winter-vacation/Cross-country-skiing

Starting point for access to the trails:

- Ettal: Ettaler Mühle, parking area.
- Oberammergau: Tennisplatz (tennis hall)
- Friedhof (cemetery)

Directions: From Garmisch, travel on route B23 toward Munich. Turn left when you arrive in Oberau, following signs to Ettal, Oberammergau and Murnau. Upon leaving Ettal, turn left onto ST2060. Follow signs to Schloss Linderhof. Paid parking is available on the right at the Ettaler Mühle.

AUSTRIA

Yes, you read that correctly, I did say Austria! Garmisch-Partenkirchen is only fifteen minutes from the Austrian border and part of the *Zugspitzarena* ski area. By purchasing a Top Snow card, you will have access to nine skiing areas, 89 lifts, and over 207kilometer of slopes.

 A *Vignette* is a toll sticker necessary for driving on Austrian highways and must be adhered to your windshield, or you will incur a severe on-the-spot fine. These are valid for various periods of time and can be purchased at gas stations, automobile clubs and anywhere displaying the sign.
- Ten-day vignette is €8.80 for automobiles and motorcycles €5.10.
- Two-month vignette is €25.70 for automobiles and motorcycles €12.90.
- Annual vignette is €85.70 for automobiles and motorcycles €34.10.

Note: Although windshield toll stickers called *Vignettes* are required for driving on many Austrian highways, you do NOT need a *Vignette* to drive to the following ski areas!

Ehrwald: My family's all-time favorite resort! A great resort with plenty of skiing and up-to-date services. Keep an eye out for *Gamsen* (mountain goats) when riding the Issentalkopf chairlift to the back side of the mountain.

Lermoos: In the last few years, this resort has expanded its ski terrain with the new Grubig II gondola, affording nice long runs in the sunshine! Confident skiers should make the *Wolfratshauser Hütte* their choice for a delicious lunch on the mountain. With its narrow, ungroomed approach, it can be tricky, but well worth it.

Shhh, it's a secret!

Where to go when it is too crowded? Yes, this is where you benefit from my local experiences! Sometimes you just can't avoid the busy skiing season and the crowds that come with it, but the following will give you some alternative choices and more time on the slopes.

Ehrwald Wetterstein: You passed this little gem on your way to Ehrwald Almbahn. With 23 kilometers (14 miles) of runs, this little resort is spread out nicely and features intermediate runs. Be sure to ski over to the *Gamsalm* for a delicious Tyrolean meal.

Directions: From Garmisch-Partenkirchen, drive toward Reutte on B23. Cross the border in Griesen and continue on B23 until you reach the end of the road. Turn left toward Ehrwald. Make another left turn near the gas station and follow signs to the Zugspitze. Continue on this road until you see a large red sign advertising the *Gamsalm*, turn right and continue on this road till you reach the small parking area of the Wetterstein Bahn.

Biberwier: This small family-friendly resort offers 10.3 kilometers (6.4 miles) of slopes with nice, wide and long runs. This is virtually crowd-free and perfect for beginners and intermediate skiers. Make sure to ski over to the Jochlift and Almlift T-bars on the back side. The *Marienbergalm* sits at the bottom of the Almlift and is a quaint and cozy cottage where you can warm up and refuel with drinks and snacks. If there is fresh snow, this back side is an untouched powder playground!

Directions: From Garmisch-Partenkirchen, drive toward Reutte on B23. Cross the border in Griesen and continue on B23 until you reach the end of the road. Turn left toward Ehrwald. Continue to follow this road, leaving Ehrwald and proceeding until you reach the cube-shaped Hotel My Tirol. Turn left into the parking area.

Berwang: Ski to the highest brewery in Austria, Hotel Thaneller.

Spend the day in Austria, skiing from Berwang to the small town of Rinnen for beer tasting and a hearty Tyrolian lunch at the Hotel Thaneller.

Begin in Berwang on the Almkopfbahn, go to the right and ski down to the bottom of the Egghof Sunjet chair, but take the Biliglift T-bar. Traverse across and ski to the bottom of Thanellerkarlift T-bar. From the top of the Thanellerkarlift, ski down about a quarter of the way and look for a path on your right. If you miss it, just repeat the Thanellerkarlift again. (It is a fun run anyway, so you might as well!) This path will end at a road, cross the road, and jump on the Panoramabahn Rastkopf chairlift. From the Ober Rastkopf, ski to the bottom of the Rinnerlift. The hotel and brewery will be across the street where you will see signs and a large hotel with a pointed cone roof. Trust me; it is well worth the effort!

Directions: From Garmisch-Partenkirchen, drive toward Reutte on B23. Cross the border in Griesen, continue on B23 until you reach the end of the road. Turn right toward Lermoos. Continue to follow B179, proceeding until you reach the Bichlbach – Berwang Almkopfbahn. Turn left into the parking area. You can also take the Regiobahn (train) from Garmisch to Bichlbach-Berwang. This takes approximately forty minutes.

Cross-Country Skiing

Just across the border and past Scharnitz, you will find the Leutasch valley, which is part of the Olympic Seefeld Region. When the cross- country skiing is less than desirable in Garmisch, this is where I go. Blessed by a unique position between the mountains, this area maintains its snow cover for a much longer period of time.

Seefeld has an outstanding, generous network with over 279 kilometers of connected trails. It is no surprise that Seefeld hosted the Nordic competitions for the Olympic Games of 1964 and 1976. In 2019, this will be the venue for the FIS Nordic World Cup Ski Championships.

Expect a fee for parking and skiing here. If you don't have equipment, there are plenty of places you can rent whatever you need.

Directions: From Garmisch-Partenkirchen, drive toward Innsbruck - Mittenwald on B2. Continue on past Scharnitz, A177. When you see the sign to Seefeld, turn right and follow signs to the *Loipe* (cross-country ski run).

3

SNOWSHOEING

This is a perfect way to get off the beaten path and immerse oneself in the beautiful snowy Bavarian mountainside.

Eibsee: Follow the trail from the parking area in a counter-clockwise direction, with the lake on your left. Before crossing the bridge, follow the snowshoe path to the right. Continue on this forest path until you reach an intersection. Turn left, following the signs to Übern Zierwald. Continue on the forest service road and reconnect to the Eibsee. You can choose to continue clock-wise around the Eibsee or turn back to parking lot. There is a large protected deer feeding area along the way.

The footpath around the Eibsee is 7.5 kilometers (4.7 miles) long and is well maintained, even in the winter months. Just be careful of icy conditions. Estimated time: 1.5 - 2 hours.

Directions: From Garmisch-Partenkirchen, drive toward Reutte on B23. Take the left to Zugspitzbahn – Eibsee. Continue on this road until you arrive at the Eibsee Lake. Paid parking is available to the right.

Wank: Depending on how long or steep you want your snowshoe experience to be, the Wank offers you the possibility of starting from the parking lot or doing a full circle from the mid-station with the gondola.

The ascent from the parking area is long and steep; the trail is approximately 1.2 miles long to the Sonnenalm.

From the mid-station, you can also follow the path to the *Esterbergalm*. Estimated time: 1.5 hours.

From the top of the Wankbahn, you can snowshoe on the plateau with the stunning views all around you.

There is even a 200-meter toboggan run prepared at the top of the Wankbahn. Sleds are available free of charge.

Find more information here: http://zugspitze.de/en/winter/prices/wank.

Directions: From the Garmisch-Partenkirchen train station, drive toward Partenkirchen on Bahnhofstrasse. Turn left on B2 (toward Munich) and follow signs to the Wankbahn, which will be on your right. Alternatively, from the train station, continue straight into Partenkirchen (Ludwigstrasse), then turn left onto Münchnerstrasse. Follow this road, turning right onto Münchnerstrasse or Schützenstrasse and then go left onto Münchnerstrasse. Follow signs to the Wankbahn on your right.

Kreuzeck: Thanks to the Kreuzeckbahn (1652m), you can snowshoe—or better yet, ski tour to the *Stuibenhütte* (1640m) in approximately 1.5 hours! This self-catering cottage is nestled beyond the trees and ski runs of the Osterfelder. Everything you bring in must also be carried out. The hut is open from 25 December – 3 April. The *Stuibenhütte* is only available for overnight stays with a reservation: info@stuibenhuette.de.

Directions: From the Alpspitzbahn, you can ski or snowshoe through the Osterfelder and proceed down the Bernadine ski run. Look for the small *Stuibenhütte* sign attached to a tree near the bottom of the Bernadine run to the right. Then enter the wooded area and proceed along the trail. The trail is well marked and has good signs.

From the Kreuzeckbahn, proceed toward the Alspitzbahn and look for the path KE5, which cuts left and traverse under the Hochalmweg. Just watch out for approaching skiers! Once you intersect with the Bernadine lift, continue on KE5 to the *Stuibenhütte*.

Directions: Kreuzeckbahn is located on Kreuzeckbahnstrasse. Turn at the light from Zugspitzstrasse, B23.

Grainau: Begin at Neuneralmweg, just above the intersection of Oberer Dorfplatz and Zugspitzestrasse where the Grainau nativity display is located. Proceed in front of Landhaus Ostler and follow the small zig-zag path up the hill. The first section is the steepest, so don't worry, it does not get harder! When you reach the top, continue straight across the road. Continue into the forest and follow the marked snowshoe trail, which will lead you up and into a secluded snow-covered forest. Along this route you will find some interactive highlights which are part of Grainau's "Fabled Mountain Forest," the *Zauberwald*. When you reach the intersection, turn right and you will connect to the forest service road. Continue along and turn right on Neuneralmweg, leading you back to the parking area where you began.

This hike is also great with lighted torches in the evening! Torches (*Fackeln*) can be purchased at most grocery stores or hardware stores.

Estimated time: 1.5 hours.

Directions: From Garmisch, follow B23 toward Reutte. Make the first left into Grainau just after the Zugspitze Camping & Schmölzterwirt Restaurant. Continue on Zugspitzstrasse until you arrive at a small, elevated 3-way intersection. Turn left here on Neuneralmweg. Continue a short way to the end of the road and you will find parking on the right.

Eckbauerbahn & Ski Stadium: This two-person gondola dating back to the 1950's will transport you up to the top in a leisurely fifteen-minute ride. From the top (1250m), you can choose your direction: Partnach Gorge, Schloss Elmau, or Wamberg, Germany's highest alpine village. Alternatively, you could take a short walk to the Berggasthof Eckbauer for lunch with a view.

Directions: Drive to the Olympic ski stadium, where you will see that the Eckbauerbahn is located on the left side of the parking area (looking at the stadium). Paid parking is available.

Partnach Gorge: From the top of the Eckbauerbahn gondola, follow signs to the Berggasthof Eckbauer and follow the zig-zag path down toward the Partnachklamm. When you reach the intersection, turn right, following signs to the Partnachklamm. Continue past the Das Graseck hotel, to the left, and follow the second sign to Partnachklamm. Go through the gorge and you will be asked to pay a small fee upon exit. If you prefer not to go through the gorge, you can cross both bridges and continue to Berggasthof Partnachalm, which will bring you down the *Hornschlittenrennen* (bobsled track). Be sure to note the gouges in the wood supports at the turns, which were made by some daring sledding team in the past.

Estimated time: 2 hours.

Elmauer Alm: From the top of the Eckbauerbahn gondola, exit and head left, following signs to Elmauer Alm and Wamberg. There will be an intersection where you can continue straight or right, both in the direction to Elmauer Alm. The path to the right is a wide forest service road, whereas the one ahead will be through the forest. The Elmauer Alm is an extraordinary hut built in 1924 and belongs to Schloss Elmau. Expect delicious Bavarian specialties with a touch of elegance here. On my last visit, my *Currywurst* was garnished with edible flowers! Continue back the way you came or follow signs to Wamberg. You will exit the path behind the hospital and can continue on to the ski stadium parking lot.

Estimated time: 4 hours.

4

SLEDDING

Whoever said that sledding, luge, or tobogganing was only for kids surely has not experienced sledding in Garmisch-Partenkirchen!

There are plenty of places to sled in the area, each one with its own element of danger or fun! Below is a list of some personal favorites.

St. Martinshütte
Garmisch-Partenkirchen

As the oldest toboggan run in Garmisch, this will provide plenty of excitement as you sled down the 2.4-kilometer trail. The only way to reach this hut is by foot.

Hut is open Wednesday – Monday 10:00-18:00 (kitchen closes at 16:00), closed on Tuesdays.

Directions: Start by following the wide path to the left of the Bayernhalle (Brauhaustr 19). When you arrive at the intersection for the *Kriegergedächtniskapelle* (war memorial chapel) and the *St. Martinshütte*, follow the path marked to the right, *St. Martinshütte-Grasberg*. Continue on this road until you reach the hut. Watch out for oncoming sledders! Once at the hut, you can enjoy the beautiful view and take a break as you build up your courage for the descent. You will sled down the same hairpin path on which you arrived until you reach the large open field. You must bring your own sleds. If you sled in the evening, bring a headlamp!

Hausberg Ski Area
Garmisch-Partenkirchen

As the longest toboggan run in Garmisch, with 3.9 kilometers of narrow and winding paths, it is considered more difficult and not recommended for the faint of heart. What makes this special are the evening *Hüttenwirt* or *Nachtrodel* (night sledding) evenings when the mountain hut remains open into the evening.

At the bottom of the Hausberg gondola tracks, you can rent a sled and purchase your tickets. The gondola will whisk you to the top of the ski area. Your toboggan fun starts to the left (away from the visible ski slope) and down a small hill. On your right you will see signs to the Bayernhaus. Veer right and follow this semi-flat path through the forest until you reach the mountain hut. Your toboggan run continues on the marked path from the Bayernhaus. Good luck!

Nachtrodel (night skiing) at the Bayernhaus is offered every Wednesday and Friday evening, complete with *Glühwein* (spiced hot wine) and traditional Bavarian music.

The Hausberg gondola is open from 17:00-20:00.

Directions: Drive to the Hausbergbahn ski station, located at the end of Alspitzstrasse.

Kramerplateauweg
Garmisch-Partenkirchen

This area is perfect for everyone, especially children!

Directions: Start by following the wide path to the left of the Bayernhalle (Brauhaustr. 19). If you have small children, just a short distance along this path is enough for a rewarding toboggan experience.

If you continue following the path, you will arrive at the intersection for St. Martinshütte. Here, you will find a wide field with plenty of sledding and a fabulous view of Garmisch near the *Kriegergedächtniskapelle* (war memorial chapel).

Eckbauerbahn
Ski Stadium, Garmisch-Partenkirchen

After an easy gondola ride up the mountain, you will enjoy a thrilling 4.9-kilometer toboggan run down the mountain and through the forest. Starting from the top of the gondola station (1230m) you will sled down the hill to your right.

Toboggans, minibobs, and snow bikes are all available to rent at the bottom of the gondola station.

Non-sledders can purchase a round trip ticket which includes the daily special at the Olympic House (in the ski stadium) for €19.50, or coffee and cake for €17.50. You can use this special ticket for the Eckbauerbahn and/or the Graseckbahn, allowing you the flexibility to enjoy a winter walk from the Eckbauer to the Graseck.

Estimated time to walk is 40 minutes.

Directions: Drive to the Olympic ski stadium, where you will see that the Eckbauerbahn is located on the left side of the parking area (looking at the stadium). Eckbauerbahn hours of operation: 9:00-16:30.

Prices: One-way €9.50, round trip €14. Discounts are given for teens and younger children. Sled rentals: €5-10. More information can be found at: http://www.eckbauerbahn.de/.

Hornschlittenrennen Route
Olympic ski stadium, Garmisch-Partenkirchen

Test your nerves of steel with this historic toboggan route where each year teams of four persons compete on large traditional alpine sleds.

Directions: At the Olympic ski stadium, follow the path to the Partnachklamm (Partnach gorge); as you look at the stadium, it is to the right. Go through the gorge and upon exiting, cross over the larger bridge to the right, and then again over a second bridge to the right, following signs to Partnachalm Berggasthof through the wooded trail.

Sleds are available for rent at the hut for €5.

Partnachklamm gorge: Open 10:00-18:00 daily. Entry fee is €4.

Partnachalm Berggasthof: Open until 18:00, but it is best to call and confirm if they are open. 08821-2615. Closed on Thursdays.

Ehrwalder Almbahn
Austria

This is by far the widest and longest toboggan path I have experienced. Imagine an entire evening of sledding down the flood-lit beginner ski slopes, only to jump back onto the gondola and keep repeating till you have had enough! With three full service restaurants at the top and bottom of the gondola, taking a break will not be a problem!

Sleds are available for rent at the bottom of the Ehrwalder Alm gondola. The doors open promptly at 18:30. There is a procedure you must follow: first fill out your form, then stand in line to pay, and lastly, you'll need to exchange a form of ID for your sled. Be sure to remember your sled numbers – you have to return the correct ones! You are permitted to bring your own sleds. If you happen to have a 365 Zugspitze Ski card, this card is valid for sledding nights.

Every Tuesday and Friday night is *Nachtrodeln* or *Rodelabend*. Night sledding runs from 18:30-21:30.

Sledding season begins the week of Christmas and lasts through March -snow conditions permitting. Cost of the gondola: €20 (adults) or €16 (with a valid day ski pass.)

Driving Directions: From Garmisch, follow Zugspitzstrasse/B23 toward Reutte. When you arrive at a T-intersection (crossing under a stone arch), turn left toward Ehrwald. Continue on Garmischer & Hauptstrasse. You will see a large statue of an elk; turn left here (Kirchstrasse). Continue on this road until you arrive at the gondola station. Estimated driving time: 30 minutes.

Gamsalm
Austria

Twice a week the beautiful *Gamsalm* mountain hut has a *Rodelabend*, night sledding, which attracts sledders, ski tour enthusiasts, as well as snowshoers. With live music and delicious food, this is a perfect snowy evening out! Every Wednesday and Saturday from Christmas until the end of March, the *Gamsalm* is open. The trails are lit, but it would be advisable to bring a headlamp.

In case you do not wish to drive, you can take a special taxi for €40 from the Marienplatz in Garmisch to the bottom of the Wettersteinbahn ski lift. You can start your ascent to the *Gamsalm* from there. Contact Taxi Helmi at +49 1712137262.

Reservations are required. You can reserve by emailing griasenk@gamsalm-ehrwald.at.

Driving Directions: From Garmisch, follow Zugspitzstrasse/B23 toward Reutte. When you arrive at the T-intersection (crossing under a stone arch), turn left toward Ehrwald. Turn left in front of the gas station and follow the signs to the Zugspitze. Continue on this road until you see a large red sign advertising the *Gamsalm*, then turn right and continue on this road until you reach the small parking area of the Wettersteinbahn.

From the parking area, walk along the path into the forest (left, looking at the mountain) and continue walking along the ski slope until you reach the *Gamsalm*. Continue farther up the ski slope for a longer descent.

Estimated time: 45 minutes.

SPRING

Springtime in Bavaria can be a fickle season! With the snow beginning to melt and the days getting longer, it is not unusual to see temperatures fluctuate from 68°F (20C) to 53°F (12C) from day to day.

The joys of living in the Alps!

5

SPRING

Highlights:

- Farmers Market - *Wochenmarkt*
- Munich Springfest - *Frühlingsfest*
- Asparagus Season - *Spargelzeit*
- St. George Market - *Georgimarkt*
- Night of music - *Gap-Live-Nacht*
- Maypole Day - *Maibaum*
- Ascension Day - *Christi Himmelfahrt*
- International Military Music Festival - *GaPa Tattoo*
- Pentecost (Whit Monday) – *Pfingsten (Pfingstmontag)*
- Corpus Christi - *Fronleichnam*

FARMERS MARKETS - *WOCHENMARKT*

Local farmers display their goods along the streets of Partenkirchen every Thursday and in Garmisch, as well as every Friday morning (about 08:00) until shortly after 13:00.

Here you can find local produce, cheeses, and delicious makings for a picnic-style lunch! There is no haggling for prices here, but be sure to ask before you touch any produce! Cash and credit cards are accepted.

MUNICH SPRINGFEST - *FRÜHLINGSFEST*
April

This "mini Oktoberfest" is much smaller than Munich's famous Oktoberfest, which is held annually in September. You will still find that many of the large breweries have tents featuring their spring wheat beers—*Frühlingwiesnbier*—and plenty of entertaining rides and games for everyone. One of the highlights of this festival is on the first of May, when the Maypole is raised in the center of the festival by locals wearing their traditional *Trachten*.

A family day is offered with discounted pricing. More details are available on the main website: http://www.fruehlingsfest-muenchen.de/index.htm#programm.

Antique lovers will delight in over 1,000 vendors selling their treasures at the largest flea market in Bavaria! This is offered the first Saturday of the Festival, so be sure to check the program schedule for more details.

ASPARAGUS SEASON - *SPARGELZEIT*
April

As the local farmer's rule dictates, *"Kirschen rot, Spargel tot"* ("when the cherries are red, asparagus is dead") – therefore, the harvest usually comes to an end by late June.

As early as April, these tender white stems are ready for harvest. Grown entirely surrounded by earth in knee high piles, they are more subtle in flavor and higher in nutrients than their green relatives. Harvested by hand, after a three-year long growth process, they are ready for enjoyment.

Spargel facts:

- During this season, an average German will indulge in this spring vegetable at least once a day.
- Over 70,000 tons of white asparagus are produced per year.
- Spargel season comes to a finish on the feast day of St. John the Baptist (24 June).
- The first document that mentions the cultivation of asparagus in the region around the city of Stuttgart dates back to the 16th century.

St. George Market - *Georgimarkt*
April

Surely you have seen St. George many times during your travels, typically illustrated by a soldier on a white horse killing a dragon with his sword. The best-known legend comes from the 13th century and is recounted in similar ways on several walking tours of Partenkirchen:

> According to the *Golden Legend*, a dragon poisoned the air of a small village. In order to appease him, the townspeople would sacrifice a lamb and a virgin. On one fateful day, the princess of the country met her good fortune: Saint George injured the dragon with his lance and freed her. Saint George then offered to kill the dragon if the entire population converted to Christianity. Since the 13th century the most widely used figure of Saint Jordi is the scene where he kills the dragon with a lance while riding a white horse. Source: www.pitt.edu.

Locally, this means that stores in historic Partenkirchen are given an exception to remain open in order to celebrate St. George (23 April).

Night of Music – *Gap-Live-Night*
April

GAP Night Live, Garmisch

With more than a dozen top bands performing throughout Garmisch, the evening promises to be filled with music and fun. Don't worry about parking because there is an excellent shuttle "party bus" included with your ticket. Find your free guide to the evening at the local tourist office.

Long Night of Music, Munich

So many styles of music in one evening! Live performances at over hundred locations such as: cafés, theatres and galleries. The special shuttle service makes it easy to explore various locations. Your ticket includes all music venues and the shuttle service. The evening begins at 20:00 and ends at 03:00.

More information on pricing and bus routes can be found at:
http://www.muenchner.de/muskiknacht/.

MAYPOLE DAY - *MAIBAUM*
May 1st

This ancient festival, which celebrates the arrival of spring with a festival and a large Maypole, is still observed in this part of Bavaria. Local *Trachten* clubs (Vereine) gather together and raise a Maypole, which is adorned with ribbons, flowers, and wreaths representing their local club.

Many of these groups will search the forests early for the perfect tree and hide it, as part of the tradition is to steal one another's maypoles! There are strict rules that you cannot damage another's Maypole, but once "captured," one can negotiate its ransom and return!

One of the most cunning thefts occurred in 2004. A twenty-meter Maypole was stolen from the top of the Zugspitze, Germany's highest mountain, by helicopter. They say that negotiations for its return went on all night and an undisclosed amount of food and beer were consumed during those negotiations!

ASCENSION DAY – *CHRISTI HIMMELFAHRT*
May

Ascension Day marks the day on the Catholic calendar when Christ ascended into heaven to take his rightful place at the right hand of God. Celebrated since 370 A D, this celebration occurs on the fortieth day after Easter, and always on a Thursday. You will see processions walking through town in the morning, with young children, all dressed in white, on their way to Church.

All businesses are closed on Ascension Day.

INTERNATIONAL MILITARY MUSIC FESTIVAL - *GAPA TATTOO*
May

Since the 1930s, music has played in the Garmisch Michael-Ende gardens (more commonly known as the Kurpark). From Mid-May through the end of September you can listen to operetta melodies, traditional Bavarian folk music, country, swing and jazz.

Be sure to check with the tourist office for a complete program guide.

Free Music Events:

Wednesdays – Brass bands in the Partenkirchen gardens (in case of rain, in the Richard Strauss Hall)

Thursdays - 17:00, "after work parties" at the Krönner Coffeehouse

Fridays – Brass bands play in Garmisch Michael-Ende Gardens (Kurpark)

Saturdays – 14:00, in the Mohrenplatz

Special Highlights:

A folklore evening is performed by the Grainauer Musikanten *Schuhplattler* in the Michael-Ende Gardens in Grainau.

MICHAEL ENDE GARDENS – *MICHAEL ENDE KURPARK*

This beautiful oasis of nature is literally parallel to the bustling pedestrian zone of Garmisch and definitely worth a visit! Beautiful lush green foliage will greet you as you wander through a grass maze, magic herb gardens, small amphitheater, and foot massage garden. With plenty of shaded, quiet areas it can also be the perfect escape to from a busy touring day. I highly recommend the Kneipp bath – go ahead, kick off your shoes and rejuvenate your feet and legs with this invigorating foot treatment! There are four ways to enter the garden: Richard Strauss-Platz, Fürstenstraße, Kongresshaus parking area, and Alleestraße.

Michael Andreas Helmuth Ende was a local Bavarian author of fantasy and children's fiction. You may be familiar with his fantasy *The Neverending Story*. Take a moment to tour the exhibition and step into his fantasy world! The exhibition is located in the Kurpark and is open daily Tuesday – Sunday 14:00-18:00. The entrance fee is €3 adults, €1 Children 6-16 years old, and €5 for the family.
The gardens are open daily from 07:30-22:00.

PENTECOST (WHIT MONDAY) – *PFINGSTEN (PFINGSTMONTAG)*

This religious celebration is observed on the fiftieth day after Easter. Whitsun, also known as the birthday of the church, is celebrated with beautiful church processions and services. This is the day when the church commemorates the day following Christ's ascension into heaven and the Holy Ghost appeared to His disciples.

All businesses and banks are closed on this religious holiday.

The *Wieskirche* (meadow church) celebrates the Monday after Pentecost with a pilgrimage of participants in traditional *Trachten*. The Wieskirche is the pilgrimage church of the Scourged Savior. It is located in the *Pfaffenwinkel,* the land of monasteries in the region of Bavaria. It is one of the most beautiful rococo interiors I have ever seen.

This 18th Century church continues to be a pilgrimage destination as the site of the miracle of the Scourged Savior. This statue, depicting the flagellated figure of Christ chained to a whipping post, was discovered by Maria Lory on March 14, 1738. She moved the statue to her farm, the *Wieshof,* when during evening prayers on June 14, 1738, the miracle took place. Moist drops coming from the statue's eyes were interpreted as tears. A UNESCO World Heritage Site since 1983, this magnificent balance of rococo art and religious testimony deserves a visit.

If your time permits, follow the walking paths for a beautiful walk along the meadows:

- Steingaden. From the Wieskirche, walk towards the parking area and turn left at the Moser Stefan. Walk between the large buildings and pick up the small walking path to your left. Continue until you intersect with a larger footpath, follow to the right until you reach Füssener Strasse. Turn right and head into the center of town. Estimated time: 4.5 kilometer, 75 minutes.
- Steingaden – Hiebler: Follow the asphalt road to Steingaden. Estimated distance/time: 5 kilometers, 75 minutes.
- Steingaden-Litzau-Wiesbaden: Mostly paved path with some gravel. Estimated time: 4.5 kilometers, 70 minutes.
- Landvolkschochschule: A great way to stretch your legs with a short walk to the church. Starting from the parking area of *the Katholische Landvolkshochschule*. Look for signs to turn left as you approach the Wieskirche. Estimated time: 1.5 kilometers, 20 minutes.
- Wildsteig – Holz – Wies –Weg: This meadow pathway will take you through the wooded area and the small towns. From the church, walk towards the parking area and at the fork in the road; take the footpath to the right. Continue and connect to the *Wiesweg* into the small hamlet of Holz. Continue until you reach the town of Wildsteig. Estimated time: 4 kilometers, 1.5 hours.

During mass you will not be permitted to tour the Church. Hours: 8:00 until 20:00. in the summer and 08:00 until 17:00 in the winter.

For a magical evening, consider attending one of the special concerts held at the Wieskirche. Information on concert dates can be found on the main website: www.wieskirche.de or directly at: www.wieskirche.de/konz2016.pdf.

Directions: Travel on B2 toward Munich. Take the left onto B23 toward Oberammergau, Ettal. Continue on this road until Steingadenerstrasse. Turn left, following signs to Wieskirche and Schloss Neuschwanstein. Follow the sign to Wieskirche and turn left onto St2559. Continue to the Wieskirche parking.

CORPUS CHRISTI - *FRONLEICHNAM*
May

Catholic tradition remains strong in Bavaria with the celebration of the Eucharist sixty days after Easter Sunday. Corpus Christi, *Fronleichnam*, celebrates the transformation of bread and wine into the body and blood of Christ. The holy day is observed on the second Thursday following Pentecost.

In Bavaria, Corpus Christi is a public holiday, which means all businesses and banks are closed. Restaurants and florists remain open.

The origins of the celebration of Corpus Christi dates back to 1209, when the nun Juliane of Liege saw a moon with a dark spot. She repeatedly had visions of Jesus reminding her that there was no special feast day for the Blessed Sacrament. In 1264, Pope Urban IV ordered that the observance would be the Thursday following Trinity Sunday. (Retrieved from http://www.timeanddate.com/holidays/germany/corpus-christi)

In Partenkirchen, the morning begins with a celebratory mass in the Maria Himmelfahrt Church. Beautiful processions are held in the streets of Partenkirchen, culminating at the St. Anton church.

Location: Maria Himmelfahrt Partenkirchen, Pfarrgasse 2

Walfahrtskirche Sankt Anton, St.-Anton-Straße 1

Seeshaupt

Just thirty minutes to the north of Garmisch-Partenkirchen, Corpus Christi processions are celebrated in the streets of Seeshaupt and, more impressively, on the Staffelsee lake.

The procession begins at the local church, proceeding through the decorated streets and then across the lake in small boats to the largest island of Wörth. The gospel and blessings are observed at four stations along the route. Definitely an impressive sight!

Information on worship times can be found on the main page: http://www.seehausen-am-staffelsee.de/.

Location: Pfarrkirche St Michael, Haupstraße, Seeshaupt.

Driving Directions: From Garmisch, follow Zugspitzstrasse/B23 toward Munich. Take exit 8 to Penzberg, turn left following signs to Seeshaupt. Follow Seeshauptstrasse until you reach the t- intersection. Turn right onto St. Heinricherstrasse. Continue on Heinricherstrasse, which becomes Buchscharnstraße. Make the first left after *Gasthaus Fischerrosl*. Follow the signs for the *Surf und Catamaranschule*. The Catamaran and surf school has a large parking area.

Note: More parking is available further up the road on your next left. Here you will also find the beautiful lakeside restaurant, *Zum kleinen Seehaus* as well as the fun beach-themed beach bar.

6

BEER GARDENS- BIERGARTEN GEMÜTLICHKEIT

The beer garden season kicks off in May, traditionally with Maypole dancing and a barrel of *Maibock*.

Maibock is a beer brewed entirely with pale *malts* for a warm golden hue. It is more aggressively "hopped" than other bocks for a refreshing finish. With 6 to 7% alcohol, it resembles its wintry bock cousins, but has a lighter color with more peppery hop flavors.

If you see it offered, try it. It will only be available during this time period.

PROST!
All German breweries must follow the "Purity Law" - *Reinheitsgebot*
The Purity law was originally enacted in 1516, just celebrating its 500th anniversary in 2016. According to the law, only four ingredients may be used:

Water, Hops, Barley and Yeast.

Chestnut Trees

Typically, you will find a *Biergarten* situated under huge horse chestnut trees. There is a valid reason for this! Since beer could only be produced during the cooler seasons (because of fear of fire when boiling the mashed grains into wort and the instability of the live yeast increasing potential bacterial risk), larger breweries began digging cellars into the banks of the Isar River to keep the beer cool during storage. Over the years, the ability to drink beer directly on the premises became popular. In the 19th century, brewers scattered gravel and planted chestnut trees above their cellars in order to provide shade and cooler temperatures, thus becoming the beer gardens we know today: chestnut trees, long tables with benches, and beer!

Beer gardens with their charming, festive feeling (*Gemütlichkeit*) are the perfect place to enjoy a summer day with friends!

> #Thanks Maximillian
> On January 4, 1812, Maximilian I, Bavaria's first king, signed a compromise decree allowing brewers to continue selling beer but prohibited them from selling any food except bread. Thus, this was the beginning of the *Biergarten* or beer garden.

Types of Beer:

- Helles: A light lager beer.
- Bockbier: Typically brewed from Christmas to Lent, with 6-10% alcohol content.
- Weissbier: Hefeweizen (yeast wheat)/Dunkelweizen (dark wheat)/Weizenbock (a stronger, barley-based lager).
- Radler: 50% *Pils* or lager mixed with 50% Sprite or 7-Up soda (very refreshing and appropriately named "biking beer")
- Russ: 50% Bavarian wheat beer and 50% clear lemon soda.

> „Ich möchte ein Bier, bitte!"
> I would like a beer, please.

Rules of the Garden – Yes, there are rules!

Since beer gardens have always been considered to be a popular meeting point, you are encouraged to share a table and start a conversation with those around you!

A true beer garden will allow you to bring your own food. Typically, these are self-service, outdoor cafeteria like places. Don't be surprised to see some folks bring their own tablecloth!

Self- service – it is all self-service, unless a table is specifically marked otherwise.

Prost! – Cheers! The idea is to create a fun and relaxed atmosphere, so feel free to toast your neighbors as much as you want! Be sure to look them in the eye when toasting.

Typical Biergarten Menu

Radi = radish
Brezn = soft pretzel
Obatzda =cheese dip
Halbes Hendl = half a grilled chicken
Hax'n = knuckle of pork
Steckerlfisch = grilled fish on a stick

7

SUMMER TOBAGGAN-
RODELBAHN

Hold on tight, it's that time when you get to defy the laws of gravity and fly down a mountain on a two-seater cart-like-sled! A fun activity for all, this summer version of sledding is tons of fun! Each cart has its own hand brakes, so you get to control the speed.

Below is a list of the best summer toboggan runs in the area:

Garmisch-Partenkirchen: 850 meters long. 41 meters high, 12 extremely steep turns means that this track offers lots of adventure!

Open mid-April to November, 10:00 – 18:00.

Prices: Adults €2.50 (1 trip), €12.50 (6 trips). Children (ages 3-14 years old) € 2 (1 trip) €10 (6 trips)

Location: Olympic ski jump area. Karl-Martin-Neuner Platz 3. +49 (0) 8821-56676.

Oberammergau. The Alpine Coaster is one of the most modern toboggan runs with speeds up to 25 mph. It is elevated above the ground with fantastic views as it wraps around the mountainside. The track is 2,600 meters long and features an altitude drop of 1,300 feet (400 meters).

Open March – November.

Prices: Adults €7, Children (6-15 years old) €4.50, kids (3-5 years old) free with adult. Children must be a minimum height of 1.40m and 8 years old to ride alone. Combination tickets (chairlift with alpine coaster) are €10.50 for adults, 7.50 for children. Multiple ride tickets are also available. For more information, you can visit: http://www.kolbensattel.de/en/summer/prices-summer.

Location: Kolbenlift, Oberammergau

Directions: From Garmisch, travel on route B23 toward Munich. Turn left when you arrive in Oberau, following signs to Ettal, Oberammergau, and Murnau. Take the second exit into Oberammergau onto Rottenbucherstrasse. Make a right on Kolbengasse shortly after passing the supermarket Tengelmann. Continue on Kolbengasse and park in the large parking area. From here, walk up to the Kolbenlift and arrive at the Alpine Coaster.

Unterammergau

The Steckenberg summer toboggan run is 650m long, with an altitude difference of 85m and includes plenty of steep turns, tunnels, and a few jumps.

Open 1 May – end October (weather permitting) Monday – Friday from 10:00 – 17:00; Saturday-Sunday and holidays from 10:00 – 18:00. Closed in case of rain.

Prices: Adults €3.50, Children (8-15) €2.50. For more information, you can visit: www.steckenberg.de/sommer/sommerrodelbahn.html.

Location: Steckenberg Liftweg 1, 82497 Unterammergau

Directions: From Garmisch, travel on route B23 toward Munich. Turn left when you arrive in Oberau, following signs to Ettal, Oberammergau, and Murnau. Continue on B23 through the tunnel and past the second exit into Oberammergau. The next town will be Unterammergau. Turn left onto Dorfstrasse as you enter town, turn left on Liftweg, and follow signs to Sommerrodelbahn.

SUMMER

8

SUMMER

Highlights:

- Asparagus Season - *Spargelzeit*
- Richard Strauss Festival
- Zugspitze Sledding – *Sommerrodeln*
- Summer Solstice - *Johannisfeuer*
- The White Night - *Die Weisse Nacht*
- Garmisch Festival Week - *Garmisch Festwoche*
- Garmisch Festival Week – *Partenkirchen Festwoche*
- King Ludwig Fires - *König Ludwig Feuer*

ASPARAGUS SEASON - *SPARGELZEIT*
April-June

Spargelzeit will continue until the feast day of St. John the Baptist on 24 June. During this period, restaurants will offer special menus featuring the glorious white asparagus *or Spargel*. If you have never tried it, this very German specialty is worth a try!

I have gone into greater detail about this white version of asparagus in the spring chapter. Enjoy this delicacy while you can.

RICHARD STRAUSS FESTIVAL
June

Born in Munich, Richard Strauss lived in Garmisch for more than forty years. Each year, one week is dedicated to this famous composer.

Tickets for each performance can range from €10 to €88. A *Festivalpass*,

Orchesterpass, or *Wochenendpass* can be purchased and will give you access to all performances for €133 to €531. The program for the festival will be available online in mid-October the preceding year. www.richard-strauss-festival.de/rsi2016/index.php/en/

ZUGSPITZE SLEDDING - *SOMMERRODELN*
June

It is not unheard of to have fresh snow in the Alps in the midst of summer. In June 2013, five meters of fresh snow covered the Zugspitze, which inspired my friend and me to do an overnight snowshoe hike!

Free sleds and sledding are offered on top of the mountain for anyone as long as there is snow. It is pretty cool to say that you went sledding on Germany's highest mountain...in the summer! In the winter months, the sledding track runs parallel to the ski slopes and you have access to the lifts. Of course, one must purchase a ticket to access the Zugspitze. Lift prices are €43.50 for adults, €34.50 for teens 16-18 years old, and €23.50 for 6-15 years old. Specially-priced family tickets are also available, making it more affordable for a day on Germany's highest mountain. For example, two adults and two children cost €117. Pricing information can be found at: www.zugspitze.de/tarife.

Be sure to capture a Zugspitze selfie in front of the summit cross! This is located on the terrace and you can download your photo from the webpage: http://zugspitze.de/en/winter/mountain/zugspitze/photostop-zugspitze.

#WEDDING
As Germany's highest mountain, the Zugspitze attracts over 500,000 visitors a year. Interestingly enough, this glorious mountain wasn't always part of Germany. In 1854, The Emperor of Austria, Franz Joseph I, gave his lovely bride Princess Elisabeth (often referred to as "Sissi,") the northern part of the Zugspitze. Only since then has it been Germany's highest peak. (Wikipedia: Zugspitze).

SUMMER SOLSTICE – *JOHANNISFEUER*
23 June

Each year the mountain peaks of Garmisch radiate fires in celebration of the summer solstice. Originally, this pagan celebration recognized the longest day of the year, but it has since been designated by the Christian Church as the feast day of St. John the Baptist.

Men, women and children will head up into the mountains early in the day to prepare their stations. As night falls, fires along the ridgelines will be lit. It is a very impressive sight to watch as the Waxenstein and Kramer mountains, which surround the Garmisch valley, begin to light up and form what appears to be a continuous chain of fire.

Unlike neighboring Austria, Garmisch honors the date no matter the weather conditions. Austria prefers to celebrate only in good weather conditions and will often feature a rain date, if necessary.

THE WHITE NIGHT – *DIE WEISSE NACHT*
July

Take a seat in the Garmisch pedestrian area at Bavaria's longest table (600m) decked out all in white. This is the annual summer party where everyone and everything is white! Join the festivities with various bands, DJ's, and restaurants serving up their Bavarian specialties. Stroll the pedestrian area (the *Fußgängerzone*) and shop until 20:00. From Chamonixstrasse to Marienplatz, this is the place to be on a Garmisch summer night. In case of bad weather, the evening will be postponed. The Garmisch tourist office will have the latest details.

GARMISCH FEST WEEKS - *GARMISCH FESTWOCHE*
July

Historically, Garmisch and Partenkirchen were two separate towns until 1936, when a short man with a thick black mustache ordered the two towns to unite as one town for the purposes of the 1936 Winter Olympic Games. Despite this legal merger, one can still observe that the towns have retained their own personalities and even their own folk costumes. Good examples of this can be seen in their summer festivals, which are held on separate weeks, because festival organizers would never dare to allow the festivities to overlap!

Get the dates here: http://www.gapa.de/festwochen.

GARMISCH FESTIVAL WEEK - *GARMISCHER FESTWOCHE*
Last week of July

Celebrated for half a century, this festival kicks off at the Wittlesbacher Park with an official gun salute and the tapping of the keg.

You will see a colorful array of traditional costumes (*Trachten*), with ladies wearing beautiful *Dirndls* and men in chamois *Lederhosen* with intricately embroidered suspenders representing different regions of the country.

The highlights during the week include:

- *Schuhplattler*: the energetic knee-slapping, hand-clapping dance performed by the men.
- *Goaßlschnalzen*: an exciting display of musically-timed whip cracking.
- *Wiagsogschneiden*: the Bavarian challenge of sawing a log in the fastest time.
- *Fingerhackeln*: grown men attempting to pull each other over a table, which is bolted to the floor, using their middle fingers in a small metal ring about 10cm in diameter.
- *Steinheben*: Men, women and, yes, even volunteers from the audience take turns trying to lift a huge stone weighing 509 pounds.

Each fest has its own program for the week with some events requiring a small entry fee.

Directions: The fest is located on Alleestrasse-Parkstrasse. Parking can be found nearby at Wittlesbacher Park (across the street from the fest), Kongresshaus on Parkstrasse, GEP Einkaufszentrum on Von-Brug-Strasse, or the smaller streets on Loisachstrasse (just a short walk away).

Reservations are not necessary, but if you would like to make one, this is the link: http://www.vtv-garmisch.de/festwoche/tischreservierung/.

These traditional Bavarian delights can be found at most fests:
Bratwurst: Grilled sausage
Currywurst: Sausage served with spicy curry sauce
Schweinshaxe: Pork knuckle
Weisswurst: White boiled sausages served with a sweet mustard (remove skin to eat.)
Hähnchen: Half chicken - rotisserie style with salty spices
Käsespätzle: Cheese noodles topped with crunchy fried onions.

PARTENKIRCHEN FESTIVAL WEEK - *PARTENKIRCHEN FESTWOCHE*
August

In August of 2015, this festival celebrated its 65th anniversary. It offers all that the Garmisch fest offers, but with more of a traditional local flare. The fest kicks off in the evening with a parade, complete with *Trachten* clubs, featuring a colorful display of the local folk costumes and a band.

Note: Please don't leave the children home for these fests! The fests are family friendly, opening in the morning and even have fun carnival-type games for the children. Things typically don't get too wild in the tents until very late at night.

In my opinion, the Partenkirchen fest is less touristy. My favorite program event is the *Goaßschnalzen*!

Directions: From the Garmisch-Partenkirchen train station drive toward Partenkirchen on Bahnhofstrasse. You can turn left on B2 (direction Munich) and follow signs to the Wankbahn, which will be on your right. Or, from the train station continue straight into Partenkirchen (Ludwigstrasse) and turn left onto Münchnerstrasse. Follow this road, turning right onto Münchnerstrasse or

Schützenstrasse and then left onto Münchnerstrasse. Follow signs to Wankbahn on your right.

KING LUDWIG FIRES – *KÖNIG LUDWIG FEUER*
August 24

When one visits Oberammergau, one cannot doubt how much King Ludwig II loved this quaint village and its people. To show respect to their beloved king, dozens of bonfires are shaped into elaborate designs and are lit at the top of the Kofel, Oberammergau's distinctive mountain. Since his mysterious death in 1888, Oberammergau's residents have annually displayed this fiery memorial. In 1946, a huge crown was added. As night falls, you begin to hear yodeling from the men high up in the mountains as they light the King's crown and fireworks illuminate the sky.

Preparation for this event begins months in advance, with the cutting and drying of the wood, and then finally it is carried up to the top of the Kofel's 1342-meter peak.

Just as dramatic a sight as the lighting of the crown is watching the *Feuermacher* (fire-makers) descend from the mountain in the dark, illuminated only by the flaming torches in their hands. It is a slow-moving procession as they carefully make their way down.

The best location to see the fires are anywhere with a view of the Kofel. Make reservations at a local restaurant and enjoy a late dinner with an unforgettable view.

9

SUMMER HIKING

With so many great hiking trails in the area, it is hard to resist the temptation of the magnificent Zugspitze. However, before you conquer Germany's highest mountain, I recommend these hiking options first.

I find that most visitors will consider these classic attractions when it comes to hiking: Partnach Gorge (Partnachklamm), the Riesersee, and maybe the Kreuzeckbahn.

All of these are wonderful and deserve to be visited, but since this book is about the lesser-known destinations of Garmisch, I propose the following alternatives.

Partnachklamm & Höllentalklamm

The Partnachklamm is a beautiful gorge carved over millennia by the raging, rushing waters of the Zugspitze glacier. The glacial waters course down the 700-meter-long (2305 feet) gorge. By the order of the Bishop of Freising, residents were permitted to use the gorge to transport wood for their local farms. With over 200,000 visitors to the Partnachklamm every year, I recommend that you try the Höllentalklamm instead.

The Höllentalklamm (1381m) is located in the village of Hammersbach (near Grainau). This gorge is only open during snow-free months (May – October) and is definitely more rugged than the Partnachklamm, but well worth the effort with unforgettable landscapes. The gorge is up to 150 meters deep with many waterfalls, huge boulders, chunks of ice, and wooden bridges providing a true sense of adventure! There is a small entrance fee of €4 for the gorge.

The new and improved Höllentalangerhütte, recently reopened in May 2015, is a great place to reward yourself with refreshments or a delicious mountain meal. It is possible to spend the night here; reservations are highly recommended.

https://www.davplus.de/hoellentalangerhuette/ersatzbau#horizontalTab2.

Estimated hiking time: From Hammersbach to the gorge entrance, 1.5 hours. Allow forty minutes to go through the gorge and another thirty minutes to reach the Höllentalangerhütte, a rest station with bathrooms, good food, and good beer. From the hut, you can continue on to the Kreuzeck (2.5 hours) or the top of the Alpspitzbahn (4 hours).

Riesersee & Eibsee

The Riesersee, a small lake with gorgeous views of the Waxenstein Mountains, was home to speed skating and ice hockey events for the 1936 Winter Olympics. The historic Olympic bobsled run was created in 1909 and today is a protected monument. A trip to the Bobsled museum is definitely worth a visit and is only a short walk to the

lake's periphery. The museum is open January – October on Wednesdays from 14:00 – 16:00.

Adjacent to the lake is a small beach area. I know, it sounds strange, but trust me it is a quick summertime escape! Here you can enjoy cocktails, swim, use the paddleboats and relax in this little oasis. There is a small entry fee.

Parking is also available at the Kreuzeck or at the Aule Alm. To get to the Aule Alm, follow the road to the left as you approach the Kreuzeck parking area. Turn left and follow signs to Aule Alm. From the parking area, follow the walking path toward Rießersee.

When looking for an even more stunning lake view, no place beats the Eibsee.

The Eibsee is an emerald green lake sitting at the foot of Germany's highest mountain, the Zugspitze. With jaw-dropping views of these magnificent mountains, this lake can be enjoyed all year long. This is the perfect place for a leisurely stroll, a bike ride, or a challenging run with a distance of 7.2 kilometer (4.5 miles) around the lake. About 1.5 hours (walking).

The lake was created by a giant rock slide and is spring fed with glacial ice melt. There are seven small islands scattered in the lake, which has depths up to 35m (117 feet). One can swim, paddleboard, rent a boat, or take the passenger boat across the lake. Paddleboat rentals are available. You must bring your own paddleboard or rent one from Island Times in Garmisch., or on site.

Kreuzeck & Alpspitze

During the summer months, the Kreuzeckbahn (1651m) gondola runs until 17:30 giving you plenty of time to enjoy the panoramic views from the top. It offers plenty of well-marked trails to follow and delicious hut restaurants within a short walking distance.

But why stop there? With the Alpspitzbahn (2628m) you will be rewarded with spectacular panoramic views of the Höllentall valley, the Waxenstein, and the Alpspitze North Face. Test your bravery and step out onto the 25 meter-long *Alpspix* glass bottom bridges. With unobstructed views deep down into the Höllentalklamm, you will understand why they describe the *Alpspix* as being between Heaven and Hell.

Exploring the area is made easier with two distinct adventure trails: the 3-kilometer Pleasure Adventure trail or the 700-meter Summit Adventure trail, featuring interesting and interactive stations around the top of the Alpspitze. The Alpspitze offers handicapped access to the adventure trails with a guided, elevated wheelchair. Just notify the attendant when you purchase your tickets for the gondola.

10

HIKING SAFELY

Hiking signs in Europe will always tell you three things:

1. Direction.

2. Duration of trail, in time.

3. Who can (or can't) be on the trail (persons, bikes, horses.) A red circle means something is not permitted.

DAV Categories for Footpaths

- Black dot/Difficult: narrow, often steep and risk of falling
- Red dot/Intermediate: narrow, often steep and some stretches with risk of falling
- Blue dot/Simple: narrow, sometimes steep but normally no stretches with risk of falling
- Yellow dot/Footpaths in the valley are mostly wide and features some inclines.

Vocabulary you should know:

- Verboten = forbidden
- Nur = only
- Lebensgefahr = life threatening
- Schnee = snow
- Fussweg = pedestrian path
- Weidebetrieb = pasture operation (cows

grazing)

- Betrieb = working

In case of emergency:

- Remain calm.
- Provide first aid if necessary.
- Call for help and wait to be rescued.
- Call 112 - it will work on any mobile phone.
- On the back of the signposts you will find a *Standort Nummer* (location number). This is your location which is registered with the emergency service system. By providing this number, emergency crews can get to you faster.

Tips for hiking:

1. Always be prepared - know the route you are taking, have a map, bring snacks and water.

2. Take breaks.

3. Respect the posted signs.

4. Check the weather.

5. Dress appropriately and bring extra layers.

6. Bring it in, take it out! Keeping the area unpolluted helps maintain these beautiful paths and keeps nature safe. So please, pick up after yourself.

Map recommendation:

Kompass 07 Werdenfelser Land mit Zugspitze 1:35000.

DAV – *Deutscher Alpenverein*

The German Alpine Association (DAV) is much more than a hiking club. With over one million members, it is the largest mountain sports association in the world. Historically, the DAV was founded in 1869 by German and Austrian climbers in the Munich area. Volunteering their time, the DAV helps build huts and maintain paths, as well as sharing their expertise with others. Geographic areas are divided into sections, with each section responsible for the shelters, paths, and huts within that area. Today, the DAV promotes mountain sports, advocates safety in the mountains, and is committed to protecting the natural environment. It has over 350 sections, 327 mountain huts, approximately 30,000 kilometers of paths and trails, and over 200 climbing structures. As a member one receives opportunities for more education and training, special discounts at the mountain lodges as well as mountain rescue.

Source: http://www.alpenverein.de/der-dav

11

DAY HIKES

Each one of these hikes will lead you to a rustic hut with a delicious meal. There is nothing more rewarding than a delicious meal with a mountain view while hiking!

Here is a list of sixteen of my favorite day hikes:

Almhütte: From the Bayernhalle, follow signs to the Kramerplateauweg. Continue following signs to the Café-Restaurant Almhütte. Try their specialty: Cream Puffs/*Windbeutel*, served only after 14:00. Estimated time: 1 hour.

Aule-Alm: This rustic Café-Restaurant dates back to 1915 and is still family-run. Starting from the Hausbergbahn, follow path which runs parallel to the train tracks. Follow the signs and path up to Riesersee. When you arrive at the Riesersee Lake, follow path (on right) along the lake towards Kreuzeckbahn. Estimated time: 1 hour.

If it is Wednesday, take a small detour to the *Bob-Museum* (Bobsled Museum). Take a step back in time and get a true appreciation for the racers and the track back in the 1900's. The museum is open from 14:00-16:00.

Or, continue on the path parallel to train tracks until you see Kreuzeckbahn. Follow directions to left, turn left again, and follow signs to Aule Alm. Estimated time: 45 minutes.

Berggasthof Almhütte: This local favorite is affectionately referred to as the "cream puff cabin" because its specialty is the deliciously fruit-filled cream puffs, which are served all day!

Across the street from the *Almhütte*, you will see a large wooden map with many suggestions for hiking. From here you can reach *St. Martinshütte*, the soldiers' war memorial, the Kramerplateau, the Kramerspitz, and the *Königsstand*.

At the trailhead, you will see the Kneipp - a fenced area with pools of icy glacial water. Make sure you experience this rejuvenating cold water treatment, inspired by Sebastian Kneipp, who believed in the restorative and healing effects of water. After a nice hike, dip your feet into this mountain fresh water and let yourself be reinvigorated! It really works.

Eckbauerbahn: Recently updated in May 2019, this new 6-person gondola will transport you to the top of the mountain while offering you one of the best views of the Olympic ski jump and the  Wetterstein mountain range! The gondola allows plenty of room for strollers or wheelchairs with its barrier free entry, plus spaces for four pairs of skis. Bikes are easily taken up the mountain with a special "bike gondola" which accommodates two bikes at a time and arrives every 6 minutes. Skiing will be offered here beginning in the 2019/20 ski season.

There are five different walking tours you can make from the Eckbauerbahn: Partnachklamm (2 hours), Wamberg (2 hours), Schloss Elmau (4.5 hours), Valley (45 minutes), and Hintergraseck (1.5 hours). A detailed map with walking tour information can be found at the gondola station.

If you are looking for a nice afternoon, without a full day of hiking, my recommendation is to purchase the Round-Trip ticket which allows you to travel on both the Eckbauer and Graseck gondolas. You will travel up the mountain with the Eckbauer gondola, follow the signs to Partnachklamm. Walk through the woods downhill till you reach the Das Graseck Hotel. Turn left and continue about 10 minutes, where you will find the Toni Bartl's Kaiserschmarnn Alm. Seriously, the best Kaiserschmarnn I have ever had! When finished enjoying your meal, return to Das Graseck and follow path behind hotel to catch the Graseckbahn.

The Graseckbahn is only a 45-minute walk from the top of the Eckbauer. This gondola, first run in 1956, is self-operated, accommodates four to five persons, and is controlled by the base station. You will arrive back in the valley and will follow the road on the left to get back to the parking area. To the right is the Partnachklamm.

The "Weisswurst lunch" is a special "in gondola" lunch which allowed you to eat your sausages on the ride up in the gondola with a custom-fitted table. These tables are currently being redesigned and should be ready for the spring/summer season in 2020. Normally, you must reserve at least two days in advance. Your ticket includes transportation up the Eckbauerbahn, *Weisswurst* lunch, wheat beer (or beverage of your choice), and transportation down the Graseckbahn or Eckbauerbahn.

Open every day 9:00- 17:00. Pricing and detailed hiking information can be found on the webpage https://www.eckbauerbahn.de/preise/

You will find the Eckbauerbahn located to the left side of the Olympic ski stadium parking area (as you are facing the ski jump).

Grainau: This quaint village is only 6 kilometers from Garmisch-Partenkirchen and situated at the foot of the Waxenstein mountains. There are many options for hiking here!

Panoramaweg: Begin from the swimming pool (Zugspitzbad) parking area and follow the small path to the right between the parking area and the houses (Gassenbichl). Cross the road and continue on Stepbergweg until Am Krepbach. Turn right and follow the path, turning left on the small bridge. Cross the road (Loisachstrasse) and proceed up the path to your right. Follow the Höhenrain-

Panoramaweg and enjoy the gorgeous views. Along the way are informational signs about the mountains and glaciers. When you reach the intersection, turn left toward the Soldiers' Memorial. Continue with the path downhill and back into town. When you reach the town, follow Höhenrainweg to the left (you will pass behind the Waxenstein Hotel), cross Eibseestrasse and continue on Baderseeweg towards the small chapel. You will reach the main road (Waxensteinstrasse), turn right and continue back to the Zugspitzbad parking area. Estimated time: 1.5 hours, 5.3 kilometers.

You can also continue straight through the intersection, returning through the Badersee. When you reach the main road, turn left on Zierwaldweg and continue till Schönangerstrasse. Turn right on Eibseestrasse and follow signs to the Badersee Hotel. Continue on the forest trail and you will arrive at the Zugspitzbahn stop in Grainau. From here, turn left and cross the street back to the Zugspitzbad parking. Estimated time: 2 hours, 6.7 kilometers.

The Badersee, 18m deep, is fed by an underground spring, which prevents it from freezing in the wintertime. See if you can spot the mermaid below the crystal-clear water.

You have plenty of restaurant choices as you stroll back into town. My favorite is the *Spatzenhaüs'l*.

Knorrhütte (2051m): This charming, rustic hut was built in 1855 and is the oldest hut in Germany's alpine region. The hut makes an ideal lunch destination from the Zugspitze!

From the SonnAlpin Restaurant, proceed downhill from the Maypole. This area is very wide open, so just head to the bottom of the chairlift, which you can easily see from the Maypole. Once there, you will follow signs to the Brunntalkopf. Don't be alarmed if you see a large yellow "gesperrt - closed" sign, as this is for the ski season! Proceed past the sign and continue to the Knorrhütte. Sometimes the trail is a "marked path" with painted red and white rectangles painted on the rocks. You will spot the *Knorrhütte* to your left.

When you return to the Sonnalpin, take the gondola up to the summit and treat yourself to a refreshing beer on Germany's "highest Biergarten"! From the summit, you can return to the parking area with the gondola, or return to the *Sonnalpin* to catch the cog wheel train.

Estimated time: 2 hours each way. Open May - October.

Note: I hiked this in June 2013, after the Zugspitze received five meters of snowfall! We were able to snowshoe down to the Brunntalkopf and from then on, the path was clear.

Königsstand: Maximillian II Joseph, King of Bavaria, declared this area the most beautiful in the Werdenfelser Land. A once a vibrant hunting area for mountain goats, it now provides royal views of the valley below.

There are several trails leading to the *Königsstand*.

Easiest: Start at the Pflegersee parking area (845m). The trail head is across from the parking area, marked by a large wooden map structure. You will follow the trail to the St. Martinshütte (1040 m). From the St. Martinshütte, you will follow the marked path uphill behind the cabin to the Königsstand (1453 m). Estimated time: 1.5 hours.

Middle: Start at the Bayernhalle (Brauhasstrasse), continue up the road (Krammerhange) and keep going until you reach the St. Martinshütte. Continue uphill behind the cabin. You will reach the "iron pulpit." If you are fortunate, and brave, this iron balcony will offer you unspoiled and incredible views. Continue on and follow the trail to *Königsstand*, not Kramerspitz (1985m).

Difficult: Start at the Pflegersee parking area (845m). The trail head is across from the parking area, marked by a large wooden map structure. You will follow the trail to the *St. Martinshütte* (1040m) for approximately fifteen minutes. After the bridge, you will cut into the trees onto the *Mauersteig*, a nondescript path and recommended only for the sure footed. Follow this path as it parallels the stream, it will continue uphill to the right to a rock wall. Here, you will find a cave with crosses where the path divides into two forks. Proceed to the right (looking at the cave), and continue to cross the rock face, then the steep grassy slope. To return, follow signs to *St. Martinshütte*, and return to the Pflegersee parking area.

Enjoy lunch or dinner at the Pflegersee restaurant or *St*. Martinshütte.

Kramer Plateauweg: A perfect hike offering

impressive views of Garmisch-Partenkirchen. There are so many trails to take; you can continue to explore this area over and over! Complete with memorial chapels honoring the memory of fallen soldiers from WWI (*Kriegergedächtniskapelle*), a *Kneippbad* (foot bath) with Father Kneipp's famous water cure above the Almhütte, and even the ruins of the haunted Werdenfels Castle (*Werdenfels Ruine*).

Directions from Grainau: Begin on Eibseestrasse and head toward the Höhenrain. After the memorial chapel, turn right at the intersection to the Kramerplateauweg.

Directions from Garmisch: From the Tourist Information, head across the Kongresshaus parking and follow the Parkstrasse/Alleestrasse (left) towards the *Loisachbrücke* – go toward the Bayernhalle. Follow path uphill, in the direction to the Werdenfels Ruins. Estimated time: 50 minutes.

Kreuzeck - Alpspitze: One of my favorite hikes and adaptable to the direction you prefer hiking - up or down.

Hochalm Hütte: A great lunch outing! This is perfect for hikers and non-hikers alike. Because the two gondolas are in the same parking area, it is easy for everyone to meet at the hut for a rustic lunch.

If you like to hike uphill, begin from the top of the Kreuzeckbahn gondola and hike to the *Hochalm*. If you prefer hiking downhill, take the Alpspitzbahn and from there, hike down to the hut. Estimated time: 1.5 hours.

Non-hikers can take the Alpspitzbahn up, and after some photo taking and exploring of the Alspix viewing platform, connect to the Hochbahn gondola, which will take them straight down to the hut.

Loisachuferweg: A refreshing walk along the Loisach River. From the Tourist Information office, go straight through the Kurpark to the exit Alleestrasse. Follow to the left along Alleestrasse, keeping the Loisach River to your right. Cross the bridge over to Maximilianssteg (Archstrasse). Estimated time: 1 hour.

St. Martinshütte: Since 1920, this hut has been the perfect spot for hikers to refresh themselves with a delicious meal and then be rewarded with a spectacular view of the Garmisch Partenkirchen valley. At 1,040 meters, it is easily accessible from the Garmisch valley and offers plenty of routes in the area. This is an excellent hike to get your legs ready for the hiking season!

The Maximilianshöhe trail begins just across from the Berggasthof Almhütte (Maximilianshöhe 15) and is perfect for families, strollers, and leisure walkers. Estimated time: 1.5 hours.

The Kramerplateauweg begins at the trail head near the parking lot of the Pflegersee Restaurant (Pflegersee, 1). This trail is more rugged with some exposed tree roots and narrow paths. It is more adventurous than the Maximilianshöhe, but not technical or too difficult. You will follow signs to St. Martinshütte. Estimated time: 1 hour.

Stuibenhütte: Although this hut is only open during the winter season (December - April), it is a great picnic destination. From the top of the Kreuzeckbahn, proceed toward the Alspitzbahn and look for the KE5 path, which cuts left and traverses under the Hochalmweg. Once you arrive at the Bernadine lift, continue on KE5 following signs to the *Stuibenhütte*. Estimated time: 1.5 hours.

Wamberg: Enjoy a beautiful hike to Germany's highest alpine meadow parish (1016m) in Germany, and treat yourself to their house specialty, *Kaiserschmarrn*!

Kaiserschmarrn is a deliciously satisfying caramelized shredded pancake served on a plate with a hearty dusting of powdered sugar. If you order this dish in Germany, it will be served with applesauce, but in Austria it is served with plum sauce. It is said that *Kaiserschmarrn* (Emperor's Mess) was the favored dish of the Austrian Emperor, Franz Joseph I.

> Supposedly, when serving this dessert to his Emperor, the servant tripped and quickly tossed all the pieces onto the plate. It was a success and the Emperor loved it.

You can reach Wamberg from the top of the Eckbauerbahn (45 minutes), or behind the Garmisch hospital, from the parking area nearest the Kainzenbad (1 hour).

Directions: Park at the Olympic ski stadium or in the parking area between the ski stadium and the hospital.

Wank Gondola: Starting out from the Wank parking area, there are so many choices for where to go!

- Philosophenweg: A fairly flat walking path is dotted with several benches dedicated to various philosophers. The trail actually begins a little way down the road you arrived on. Walk down the Wankbahnstrasse and turn right at the Schützenhaus. Just behind the building, you will find the trail head. Follow the path toward Farchant. When you reach Farchant, you can continue to the right toward the *Kuhflucht* waterfalls or stop at Da Nico's Pizzeria. This path is stroller friendly. Estimated time: 45 minutes each way to Farchant.
- Panorama: A very nice mountain restaurant and terrace-café with a great view. The Berggasthof Panorama features locally produced Bavarian specialties and Hacker Pschorr beer. Facing the Wank gondola station, head to the left and begin your path at the marked trail map station. Look for a large wooden structure with a map and suggested trails. Follow the marked trail up to Panorama. Estimated time: 15 minutes.
- *Esterberga*lm (1262m): This lovely little hut is nestled between the Wank, Fricken and Krottenkopf mountains. It features hearty Bavarian dishes, delicious Kaiserschmarrn and beer from Ettal Abbey. You can reach this hut from the mid-way station (1.5 hours) or the top of the Wank Gondola station (1.5 hours). Just follow signs to the *Esterbergalm*.
- St. Anton: Facing the Wank gondola station, head to the right and follow the path to Partenkirchen. Along the way you will discover the hidden gem, Franziskanerkloster St. Anton, and the Stations of the Cross.

Werdenfels Ruins: Castle ruins dating back to 1219, where witches were once burned. Even the locals say it's haunted. Estimated time: One-hour trail from Kramer-Plateauweg, following signs toward the Pflegersee.

Directions: From Garmisch-Partenkirchen take B23 toward Munich. Turn left on Thomas-Knorr-Strasse, following signs to Pflegersee. Continue until you see parking on the right. Follow hiking signs to Burgruine Werdenfels. The *Werdenfelser Hütte* (795m) offers light snacks and cakes. On Sundays and holidays a special meal is offered.

Zugspitze: Don't panic, I am not suggesting that you summit this in one day, although many have accomplished this feat from the Austrian side! By using either the Zugspitzbahn (cog wheel train) or the gondola, you can enjoy panoramic walks at the top.

With three restaurants and two countries to choose from at the top, you are certain to find something delicious!

Oberammergau

Just a thirty-minute drive from Garmisch-Partenkirchen are the Ammergau Alps. This mountainous area is full of unspoiled nature. As you wind up the mountainside, imagine Emperor Ludwig's horse genuflecting three times at the current site of the Ettal Abbey. The legend states that after his horse went down on bended knee, he saw light emanating from the horse's forehead, which to Ludwig was clearly a sign from God. He promised to return from Italy and commissioned the Abbey to be built. He brought with him a statuette of the Virgin Mary from the House of Pisano, which remains a focal point of the Abbey.

Kofel (1342m)

The Kofel is Oberammergau's signature mountain. Here are two different routes to choose from, and the most common is to start from the cemetery parking.

You will begin your hike by crossing the *Kälberplatte* meadow and following signs to the Kofel. Estimated time is 1.5 hours. To return, you can retrace your steps or follow the *Königssteig* route.

Directions: From Garmisch, travel on route B23 toward Munich. Turn left when you arrive in Oberau, following signs to Ettal, Oberammergau, and Murnau. Take the first exit into Oberammergau and follow Ettalerstrasse into town. Cross the bridge to your left when you reach the Hotel Böld. You will be on Koenig-LudwigStrasse. Make your first left when crossing the Ammer River. Continue on Malensteinweg until you reach the *Friedhof* (cemetery). You will find the Döttenbühl parking area just beyond the Oberammergau cemetery at the trail head.

From the *Kolbenalm*, you can hike from the parking area. The estimated hiking time is 1.5 hours to the Kofel.

Kolbensattel (1270m)

The Kolbensattel is Oberammergau's ski area and an excellent family hike for several reasons. One, the hike is pleasant and can be done in an hour. At the top you will find the *Kolbensattelhütte*, where you can enjoy a nice meal as well as an interactive play area for the kids. Getting back down the mountain couldn't be more fun with the choice of the chair lift or the new Alpine Coaster! Tickets for the chair lift or coaster can be purchased from the *Kolbensattelhütte*.

If you prefer Italian cuisine, *Evi's Wankalm* is very good and the thin, crispy pizzas are delicious!

Directions: From Garmisch, travel on route B23 toward Munich. Turn left when you arrive in Oberau, following signs to Ettal, Oberammergau, and Murnau. Take the second exit into Oberammergau, Rottenbucherstrasse. Make a right on Kolbengasse, shortly after passing the supermarket Tengelmann. Continue on Kolbengasse and park in the large parking area. From here, you can walk up to the Kolbenlift.

Laber (1684m)

The Laber with its nostalgic gondola allows you easy access to the top, where you can enjoy views of the Ammergau, Wank, and Wetterstein mountains. Hiking can begin from the valley or from the top of the mountain.

Directions: From Garmisch, travel on route B23 toward Munich. Turn left when you arrive in Oberau, following signs to Ettal, Oberammergau, and Murnau. Take the first exit into Oberammergau onto Ettalerstrasse. Make a right on Rainenbichl and continue on the path. You will pass through the NATO School area and turn right on Ludwig-Lang-Strasse. Turn left on Himmelreich (WellenBerg). There will be a parking area to your right and signs to the Laber from this area.

From the WellenBerg parking, follow hiking signs to Soilasee. You will reach a point in the trail where you will choose the Labersteig über Schartenkopf *nür für geübte* (only for experienced hikers), or the gentler pass to the Soilasee, a lake which is typically dry during the summer. Estimated hiking time is indicated on the signs.

From the top of the Laber, you can do a nice hike to Ettal. Follow signs to Ettaler Manndl. Keep to the left at the junction, past the Soilasee and back to the top of the Laber. Estimated time: 2 hours.

FOUR UNFORGETTABLE OVERNIGHT HIKES

Most of these longer hikes can be done in one day. However, by adding an overnight stay on the mountain, they become truly memorable.

King Ludwig's *Schachenhaus* (1866m)

Commissioned by King Ludwig II of Bavaria in 1869 and completed in 1870, the *Schachenhaus* became the King's summer residence. Each year, on August 25th, the King celebrated his birthday in this stunning Alpine setting.

Make sure you visit the Botanical Alpine Garden, with over 800 species of alpine high elevation plants from all over the world. Open from mid-June to mid-September, daily from 08:00 to 17:00. Admission is €2.

There are two recommended ways of reaching the *Schachenhaus*:

1. Partnachklamm – From the Olympic Ski Stadium parking, follow the signs to the Partnachklamm. You will go through this magnificent gorge. When you exit the Partnachklamm, you will take the bridge on the right over the Partnach River. Do not take the second bridge over the river. Proceed from the bridge straight towards the woods, where you will see hiking signs to Schachen via Kälbersteig (#727). Continue up a steep, narrow trail for approximately three hours. Halfway, you will intersect with the forest road *Königsweg* (king's path), turn right and follow this larger path to the *Schachenhaus*. You can return along the same route, or down through the Reintal valley. From the *Schachenhaus* gazebo, follow signs to the *Oberreintalhütte*, you will descend down a steep rocky path with steel ropes for support. Although not technical, it is uneven and steep. Once you arrive at the *Bockhütte*, you will continue on the forest road

along the Partnach River back to the Olympic ski stadium. Estimated time for return via the *Bockhütte* is 3.5 hours.

Estimated time: 4.5 hours, 18.8 kilometers. Difficult, with an ascent of 1408 meters.

2. Elmau – The King's Route

What better way to go to the *Schachenhaus* than on the same path which King Ludwig used to ride to in his horse-drawn carriage?

From the parking lot in Elmau, you will start on a nice flat forest road, following the Elmauer creek for one kilometer. Continue on the forest road, which is slightly uphill, then after 100 meters go right and follow the signs to *Wettersteinalm*. By the way, the *Wettersteinalm* is famous for their *Kaiserschmarrn*, so be sure to try some! Continue following this path for approximately five kilometers till you reach the *Schachenhaus*. You will return the same way.

Estimated time: 3.5-4 hours, 20 kilometers. The path is medium difficulty, with an ascent of 1079 meters.

Directions: From Garmisch take B2 toward Innsbruck - Mittenwald. Exit to Schloss Elmau at Klais. Continue to follow the road to Schloss Elmau. As you arrive, do not drive to the hotel, but continue straight ahead; you will reach a parking area.

The hut is open from June to mid-October (weather permitting).

An overnight stay in a private room is €17 for adults. There are two single rooms, two double rooms, two triple rooms, and one quadruple room. Cost for staying in the large dormitories is €12 (adults), €6 (children). There are two dormitories for twelve persons each, and one for twenty-six persons. No dogs are allowed.

A buffet breakfast of cereal, coffee, tea, sausage, cheese, jam, and bread (all local products) is available for €8.

For reservations contact +49 (0) 172 8768868 or online at: www.schachenhaus.de/index.php/buchungsanfrage.

Meilerhütte 2366m

Just another 500m of elevation from the *Schachenhütte*, nestled high on the Dreitorspitzgatterl, between giant rock faces, sits the stone-walled *Meilerhütte*. Built in 1898 by Leo Meiler, and renovated in 1998, this special hut is worth the effort even with its steep and rocky approach. The views from the top are amazing!

Due to its unique position on the Dreitorspitze, energy for the hut is generated from the wind and sun. Today, it assists the German Alpine Association with its research into alternative energy sources.

A small deviation from the path will take you to the Frauenalpkopf (2352m). You can cross over the grass field to the cross, where you will reconnect to the main path.

For your return, you can repeat the trail you arrived on or choose to follow the Teufelsgsaß into Oberreintal. This is a steep descent aided by steps and cables. It is not technical and harnesses are not required. From the *Schachenhaus*, follow the path to the Belvedere viewpoint and gazebo. Follow the signs to *Bockhütte*, a perfect place to rest your wobbly legs. From the *Bockhütte*, you will follow the forest road along the Partnach River back to the Olympic Ski Stadium in Garmisch. Estimated time: 3.5 hours.

Estimated time: 1.5 hours (Schachen to Meilerhütte). Total time: 6 hours (Garmisch - Meilerhütte). The path is steep and has stretches with shale, so it is recommended that only sure-footed hikers with good hiking shoes take this path.

This hut is open from June - October.

An overnight stay in a room is €19 for adults (over 19 years), €17 for youth (7-18 years) and €15 for children (up to 6 years). Cost for staying in the large dormitories is €17 (adults), 13 (youth), and €10 (children). Note: with a DAV membership, you will receive a €10 discount per person. No dogs are allowed.

Meals are provided, pay as you go.

Reservations are possible by calling +49 171 522 7897. Reservations by email are only possible when the hut is closed: info@alpenverein-gapa.de. More information can be found on the web page: http://www.alpenverein-gapa.de/?id=119.

Knorrhütte 2052m

Before the Zugspitze cable car was installed, this mountain hut was the only refuge available to hikers seeking to conquer Germany's highest peak, the Zugspitze. It provided a mere three sleeping places. Now, 150 years later, it can accommodate 120 persons. The *Knorrhütte* sits just below the Zugspitze and the *Brunntalkopf*, which is the perfect spot to spend the night for those ascending the Zugspitze or for those who wish to hike into Ehrwald, Austria over the *Gatterl* (border crossing).

Three recommended ways to reach the *Knorrhütte*:

1. Top of the Zugspitze gondola: Take the gondola or cogwheel train up to the *Sonnalpin* (2576m) and hike down via the Zugspitzplatt. Total hiking time: 1.5 hours.

2. Garmisch Olympic ski stadium (800m) and the Reintal valley: The *Reintalangerhütte* (1357m) is the second *Hütte* along the way and provides a great stopping point. Total hiking time: 7-7.5 hours.

3. Ehrwald, Austria: Ascend with the cable car to Ehrwalder Alm (1502m) and follow signs to the Gatterl (2020m). Total hiking time: 3.5 hours.

The *Knorrhütte* is open from May – October.

An overnight stay is € 28 (private bedrooms), € 22 (dormitory); € 6 (emergency overnight).

Sleeping accommodations: 6 dormitories (1x7 person, 1 x 12-person, 2 x 13 persons, 1 x 18 persons, 1 x 22 persons); 2 x 4 beds, 3 x 7 beds; and a winter room with 4 beds.

A buffet breakfast (cereal, coffee, tea, sausage, cheese, jam, and bread) with local products is available for the price of €8.

Contact information for an overnight stay: +49 151 14443496 or online at:
www.davplus.de/knorrhuette/kontakt.

Weilheimerhütte (Krottenkopfhütte) 1956m

"The best kept secret," according to my friend, Tom Sheaffer, an outdoor
enthusiast and expert guide. Recently awarded the "So taste the mountains – *So
schmecken die Berge*" seal of approval, this hut features local products from
within a 50-kilometer radius. The food is fresh, local and delicious! It is among
one of only 100 huts to receive this special award for the best food and drink on
the table.

There are many ways to reach this hut, and with the Kompass 07 map, you can
choose the route you prefer. All trails are marked very well, and there is little
chance of getting lost. The following are just a few suggested routes:

Wankbahn (1780m): From the Wank (summit or mid-station), follow signs to
Esterbergalm, then onto Weilheimhütte. The path gets very steep towards the
end (I have chosen to return this way instead). You might be rewarded with
fields of grazing horses! Estimated time: 3 hours.

Eschenlohe (652m): By taking the train to Eschenlohe, you can do a complete
loop and return to the Wankbahn parking lot or continue into Garmisch. In
Eschenlohe, follow the marked trail to Asamklamm, then continue on the forest
road until you reach the *Krüner Alm* (1621m). Enjoy a nice break and then
continue following the marked signs to Weilheimer Hütte.

Estimated time: 5 hours. I recommend you wake up early to see the sunrise from
the cross station – it is unforgettable!

Hut is open from mid-May until mid-October (Pentecost to Kirchweih Sunday).

An overnight stay is €18 (dormitory), €20 (shared room), and €20 (private
room). Discounted prices are given to DAV members and children. Sleeping
accommodations: 3 dormitories (each sleeps 12), 1 dormitory (sleeps 5), 1x 2-
person room, 1x 4-person room, and 3x single rooms.

The meals are delicious and you have the opportunity to purchase some local products to take home.

Reservations are possible by calling +49 170-270 8052 or +49 08825 2023.

More information is available on the website: www.dav-weilheim.de/content/weilheimerhuette.html.

13

CASTLE TO CASTLE
LINDERHOF TO NEUSCHWANSTEIN
Overnight hike - 2 days

If you were asked me to name my most memorable hike, hiking from Linderhof castle to Neuschwanstein would be it! Hiking from one iconic Bavarian landmark to the next gave me a sense of accomplishment, which was evident in my ear to ear smile on the Marienbrücke!

Logistically, I pre-parked a car at Schloss Neuschwanstein the night prior. This allowed our group to return without having to rely on any public transportation. On the day of the hike, you can either drive to Schloss Linderhof or take the public bus from Garmisch train station to Oberammergau and then bus 9622 to Schloss Linderhof. Although the first hiking day is short, you should start your day early. I recommended the Kompass 05 map.

Day 1:

This hike begins at Schloss Linderhof (900m) and ends at the Kenzenhütte (1278m). There is an optional ascent to the Grubenkopf (1839m), approximately 1.5 hours, which offers fabulous views. When you arrive at the Kenzenhütte, there are additional hiking routes to explore with a lake and waterfall nearby, which are worth visiting.

This is the only Hütte where one can spend the night between these two castles. It is a beautiful, charming and privately-owned hut. Reservations are a must.

Hiking directions: The trailhead is to the left of the gift shop (moving away from the castle). Don't forget to snap some photos in front of the castle before your hike begins! Follow the Via Alpina signs to E4- Bäckenalmsattel (2.5 hours) / Kenzenhütte (3 hours)/ Hochplatte (5 hours). Most of this route will be a forest path with forest road and low shrubs. If time permits, take the small detour to the Grubenkopf. Continue to follow signs to the Kenzenhütte.

Estimated hiking time: 4-5 hours.

Day 2:

Starting early from the *Kenzenhütte*, you will follow the signs to the Gumpenkar and the Gabelschrofsattel (1.5 hours). The trail leads past the Kenzen waterfall into the *"Gasse" (narrow trail)* and over the saddle. This trail is mostly rocky with many large boulders and steady climbs up with several hairpin bends to the Kenzensattel Pass (1650 meters).

After walking down a rocky path into the Gumpen valley, several trails converge. Continue on the Via Alpina and follow the left-hand path towards the west. Further to the left, the trail follows the Fensterl. You will reach a sign and a decision to make – the *Fensterl* left (30 minutes) or Geiselsteinsattel (3/4hr)/ Gabelschrofsattel (1.5h)/ Wankerfleck (2.5h). I chose the 30-minute trail. It will be a steep climb up pure shale with a tricky rope climb over large boulders, but completely worth it when you reach the "window," the *Fensterl*, and look back through it over the valley. Note - This is an exposed area secured with ropes.

If you follow the Gaelschrofensattel, an easier route, you will continue downhill to the Schwangauer basin. This trail will eventually widen out once you are out of the wooded area.

Both trails will continue to the Pöllat gorge and the Bleckenau, the original hunting residence of Emperor Maximilian. This is a perfect place for a quick rest and refreshment! From here, it is only another hour on a wide forest road! Follow signs to Marienbrücke (Queen Mary's Bridge). Congratulations, you did it!

Estimated hiking time: 7-8 hours.

Accommodation rates are €29 (breakfast included) or €38 (with breakfast and dinner). Children €18- 24 Sleeping accommodations: 3 dormitories (sleeping 24, 16 or 6 beds), 2x 4-person room, 1x 3-person room, 3x 2-person room. More information available on the *Kenzenhütte* website: www.berggasthof-kenzenhuette.de/.

In the 1850's, Holy Roman Emperor Maximilian II honored his beloved wife, Marie, with the "Marienbrücke.". This iron bridge was built high over the Pöllat gorge, so that she could pursue her love of mountain climbing.

14

MITTENWALD

HUT TO HUT HIKE

Overnight hike - 3 days

This truly memorable hiking experience in the Karwendel mountain range is less than thirty minutes from Garmisch-Partenkirchen.

Logistically, I parked in Krun and took bus #9608 from the Café Kranzbach to the Mittenwald train station. From the train station, you follow signs to the Karwendelbahn (a pleasant fifteen-minute walk).

Day 1:
Mittenwald (930m)-Dammkarhütte (1667m)-Hochlandhütte (1623m)

This hike begins at the Karwendelbahn parking area (930m) and finishes at the rustic family owned *Hochlandhütte*. At the day's end, you will be able to appreciate your hiking journey as you watch the sun setting on the Tiefkarspitze and Karwendelspitze.

From the parking area proceed across the street via the underground passage way and follow signs to *Dammkarhütte* (#280). You will intersect with trail #271; continue on to *Dammkarhütte*. This will be a quick ascent with a scenic glimpse of the Mittenwald valley. Make note of the next intersection, #262, to *Hochlandhütte*, as you will have the option to return here after lunch at the *Dammkarhütte*.

After a well-deserved break, you can return to the aforementioned intersecting trail #262 and continue to the *Hochlandhütte*, or if you are feeling more adventurous and looking for a challenge, I recommend you continue on trail #270 behind the *Dammkarhütte* to trail #363 over the *Predigstuhl*. Note, this is recommended for confident and sure-footed hikers. You will encounter scree, narrow trails, large rocks with cable ropes. Upon arriving at the *Predigstuhl*, you will have a jaw-dropping view and understand why this is called the preacher's sermon chair!

The recommended route is to return to the intersecting trail #262 and connect to #260 to the *Hochlandhütte*.

Estimated hiking time: 4-5 hours.

Accommodation rates are €10 (DAV members, 26+ years old), €6.50 (DAV members 19-25 years old), €5.00 (DAV members 7-18 years old), free for children under 6 years (with DAV membership). Non-members: €20 (26+ years old), €16.50 (19-25 years old), €15.00 (7-18 years old), €5.00 under 6 years old. Breakfast buffet available for €9.00 (€5.50 children up to 12 years old). Sleeping accommodations: total of 41 beds. More information available on the *Hochlandhütte* website: http://www.sektion-hochland.de/ Reservations mandatory. +49 174 9897 863.

Day 2: *Hochlandhütte* (1623) to *Soiernhaus* (1613)

Starting early from the *Hochlandhütte*, you will follow signs to *Vereiner Alm* (#266). A quaint little hut nestled in the middle of a pristine pasture, an excellent spot for lunch. Try the apple cake here – it was delicious! Before starting out, be sure to dip your feet into the cold stream, it will help rejuvenate you and prepare you for the next four hours.

Continuing onto the *Soiernhaus*, follow trail # 360/361. After a fast ascent, you will enter a vast valley of green where you will most likely be able to spot some *Gams*. As you begin to make your way down the rocky path, the sight of the *Soiernsee* will keep you motivated.

Today, the *Soiernhaus* is a very charming mountain hut with a festive evening atmosphere. In 1866, King Ludwig II would frequent the area during his hunting trips. He had the original *Soiernhaus* built along the banks of the *Soiernsee*.

Estimated hiking time: 7 hours.

Accommodation rates are €10 (DAV members, 26+ years old), €6.50 (DAV members 19-25 years old), €5.00 (DAV members 7-18 years old). Non-members: €20 (26+ years old), €16.50 (19-25 years old), €15.00 (7-18 years old). Breakfast buffet available for €9.00 (€5.50 children up to 12 years old). Sleeping accommodations: 4 dormitories, total of 60 beds. More information available on the *Soiernhaus* website: http://www.alpenverein-hochland.de/soiernhaus. Phone: +49 171 5465858.

Open from mid-May till mid-October.

Day 3:

Soiernhaus (1613) to Krun (581)

Follow #364 in the direction of Krun. Most of this path was a large forest road, which can be a bit anti-climactic compared to what you have already hiked. This route will take you to the adorable white *Fischbachalm*, where you just might enjoy a short break.

You will then arrive into Krun.

Estimated hiking time: 4 hours.

Recommended maps: Kompass 26 *Karwendelgebirge* and Mittenwald *Panoramawanderkarte*.

15

HISTORICAL PARTENKIRCHEN

Often overlooked by many, this picturesque side of town is steeped with history and is 800 years older than Garmisch. Recently revitalized with new shops and restaurants, its half-kilometer road of multi-colored buildings, Ludwigstrasse is decorated with beautiful luftmalerei and makes for an enjoyable day. It would be a shame not to dedicate some time here.

Begin your day at *Sebastianskirchel*. This small yellow ochre chapel sits at the lower end of Ludwigstrasse, on the site of the former plague cemetery. The chapel was built in 1637 and is dedicated to victims of the Plague. Although St. Sebastian did not live during the time of the plague, he is recognized as the patron saint of the plague because his wounds resembled those of a plague victim. Quite often, this chapel is open and you should take a look inside. On the entry façade is a fresco of the Four Horsemen of the Apocalypse (Plague, War, Famine and Death) painted by Joseph Wackerle.

According to legend, a Shepard boy was bringing his goats home at the end of the day on Sunday, 19 October 1634. He was feeling ill and fell to his death on the Geissbbrueckerl (goat bridge) on Faukenstrasse. The citizens of Partenkirchen vowed to ring the church bells each Sunday at 4pm if they did not have to mourn another victim to the plague. To this day, you will hear the church bells at 4pm on Sunday.

Strolling up the cobblestone streets, you are walking on the original Roman road which allowed a direct trade route from Augsburg to Venice, Italy. Stables were under the arches on your right-hand side. If you were traveling from Augsburg, you likely had a horse and would need to exchange it for a strong ox in order to make it over the difficult Brenner mountain pass. And visa-versa for those coming from the Brenner pass on their way to Augsburg.

On the left side of the street, between houses #78 and #76 you can see the Patron Saint of Garmisch: Saint Martin. Saint Martin is strongly associated with the legend of the cloak. According to legend, Martin, a Roman soldier who converted to Christianity, comes across a beggar and cuts his military cloak in half to share it with the scarcely-dressed beggar. That night, Martin dreamed of Jesus wearing the cloak. Another version states that Martin woke to find his cloak restored whole again.

House #74 has been home to the old rope-making trade for several generations.

As you stroll up the street, be sure to look up where you will see beautiful luftmalerei on the building facades. Each one will typically depict three themes: religion, type of business, and sometimes something about the owner.

Continuing up the cobblestone-street, look above the Sparkasse bank building. This fabulous fresco tells the story of Emperor Ludwig's gift to the church in Ettal. Fulfilling a vow to select a place of strategic importance on his return from Italy, it is said that the Emperor's horse genuflected down onto one knee on the site of the original church foundation. The Emperor took this as a sign and it would be the foundation for a new church. The prolonged construction of 17 years prompted the Emperor to visit the building site. Dismayed, he found the beautiful statue abandoned in a wheelbarrow and the workers indifferent to the construction of the church.

The *Schäfflertanz* fountain, located in front of the Drei Mohren Hotel-Gasthof, commemorates the final days of the plague, when in an effort to encourage citizens to come out of their homes for fresh air, members of the schäffler (coopers) danced in the streets with pine covered copper rings.

The Werdenfelser Hof has been owned by Augustiner Brewery since 1935. Originally, this building dates back to the 16th century when it was a pub, saloon and guesthouse. If you come here for dinner, you will be treated to a Schuhplattler performance!

House #55, on your right, features three historic moments for Garmisch-Partenkirchen: Emperor Barbarossa falling to his knees in front of Henry the lion Duke of Saxony in 1176, the erection of the summit cross on the Zugspitze in 1851, and the Olympic Winter Games of 1936.

Stop for a coffee or a pastry at the oldest bakery in Bavaria, Joseph Kratz, over 240 years old! The croissants will melt in your mouth. #52 Ludwigstrasse.

On the corner, the Ludwig Pharmacy features a very famous and historical protected painting by Heinrich Bickel. The fresco features allegorical figures from medical sciences. The pharmacy itself is over 100 years old.

The Werdenfelser Museum is the perfect escape to local history. Although the museum has a wonderful collection, I recommend you pay the small fee to enter and focus on the first room to the left. The Zugspitze cross, erected in 1851, required 28 people to carry each piece of the cross and hike up through the Reintal valley to the peak of the Zugspitze. Each piece was made of gilded iron and measured 14 feet long. This cross remained on the summit until the 1970's when it was replaced with a shorter cross due to lightening. It is complete with a soldier's bullet holes from the 1940's. There are several historical DVD's available to watch by request. Although they are in German, I suggest that you watch *IV. Olympische Winterspiele 1936*. I am not going to sugar coat it: this is history and we all know what was happening during this time, so although it might be bit chilling to watch, it is interesting to see this piece of history.

On a brighter note, I recommend the film: *Ski World Cup 2011*. This film features the opening ceremony in the ski stadium as Garmisch was bidding for the 2018 Olympics. The film does a great job capturing the spirit of the event.

Zum Rassen, #45 was one of the original breweries of Garmisch-Partenkirchen, the "Risen". This oldest and most historic of inns in Partenkirchen is named after Count Russo of Andes's. He is depicted on the large mural on the façade. Today, the massive back room with its original wooden floors is home to a

Bavarian rural folk theatre. Underneath its wooden floors was where the beer was stored and kept cool. And yes, you can take a peek inside – just go past the large doors near the restrooms!

The Parish chapel was completely destroyed in the 1864 fire. Several years later a neo-Gothic style parish church was built. Only one painting remains from the original church, a The Ascension of Mary by Litterini (1731). You can find it on the left side of the church.

Chocolaterie Amelie is my favorite chocolate store! Hopefully, you have had lunch by now and can enjoy some dessert. Each month features a special truffle. Fortunately, they also have a shop in the pedestrian area of Garmisch (in case you can't get over to this side of town).

You can't miss this next house, #27. It has a bay window which was quite uncommon for this time and did not adhere to the local architecture. I have been told that it was built by a very wealthy architect, possibly copying the Golden Dachl of Innsbruck. What makes this building so interesting is the owner's subtle message around the side of the building. Roughly translated, it says: *"with each day I grow old, grows the number of those who can kiss my a--"*.

Almost at the end of the street, on the left you can see another magnificent fresco by Heinrich Bickel above the Gasthof Fraundorfer. It depicts a traditional country wedding. I can recommend this restaurant for lunch or dinner; the portions are quite generous and the food is good! Plus, you will be entertained by live accordion music as well as the Schuhplattler dancers during evening meals.

At the end of the road sits the Alte Haus - "old house"- which dates back to 1772. This house was spared by both fires of 1811 and 1865.

If time permits, take a 30-minute stroll to get a beautiful view of Partenkirchen from above. Tucked in between the Alte Haus, #8 and Wittman Shoe store, #6 are stone steps. At the second group of steps, follow the stone path to the left which parallels Ludwigstrasse. When the path ends, take a sharp right and follow the paved road, Römmerstrasse. Continue on Römmerstrasse until you see a grassy area with bench on the right. Return the way you came.

AUTUMN

16.

Autumn

Highlights:

- Oktoberfest
- Almtreib
- Eng valley

OKTOBERFEST
September

How does one write about
Bavaria and NOT mention the
biggest *Volksfest* (people's fair)
in the world?

Munich held its first Oktoberfest
on October 12, 1812. The festival
was in honor of the Crown Prince
Ludwig's (who later became
King Ludwig I) marriage to
Princess Therese of Saxony-Hildburghausen. All of Munich's citizens were
invited to join the celebration, which was held in a large field just outside the
city, the *Theresienwiese* (Therese's meadow).

Originally, the festivities were to last seven days, but due to the late arrival of
Princess Therese's brother, the celebration was extended to a full fourteen days.
The festivities typically ended with an exciting horse race.

Although the horse race is no longer held, the Oktoberfest is still celebrated
every year and draws over 6 million visitors, with more than 60,000 hectoliters
of beer consumed. (A hectoliter equals 26.41 U.S. gallons.) Yes, that's
1,584,600 U.S. gallons! But why is the Oktoberfest held in September? Simply

because the evenings are warmer and visitors are able to enjoy the gardens outside the tents for longer periods of time! The Oktoberfest concludes on October 3rd, German Unity Day.

OIDE WIESN – not to be missed!

Since its 200th anniversary, the Munich Oktoberfest has added the *Oide Wiesn* (the Old Meadow – in the local Bavarian dialect). This is a tribute to the original Oktoberfest – complete with period costumes, traditional games and carousels dating back to the 1900's. Beer is served in the original gray stoneware mugs, keeping your beer colder and fresher longer.

You will pay a small fee to enter this area. It is a great way to step back into the past and temporarily escape the more modern and sometimes crazy Oktoberfest.

Reservations for the Oktoberfest may be made as early as January. All reservations must be made by fax or email request, which can be found online at www.oktoberfest.de. Because each tent handles its own reservations, I recommend you study the website to choose which tent you prefer. There are fourteen large tents and plenty of smaller tents, each with a specific ambiance, specialty, and beer. You will find all six of Munich's breweries here: Augustiner (established in 1328), Löwenbräu (1383), Spaten (1397), Hacker-Pschorr (1417), Hofbräu (1589), and Paulaner (1634).

Typically, the fee per person with a reservation is €30 and includes two liters (two Maß and a half roast chicken). I like to reserve the "happy hour" time of 15:00. Usually, weekend evenings are hard to secure.

If your table is decorated with pretzels and a delicious array of radishes, cheeses, and salamis – know that this is NOT included in your reservation. You will be charged extra for whatever you consume! Simply ask your server to remove it.

If you choose not to reserve a table, know that if the reserving party does not show up within 30 minutes of their reservation, the table is considered available and you may stay!

If you do not have reservations, I have two suggestions:

1. Ask to share a table with someone.

2. Look for a reserved table and assure the waitress right away that all you want is a beer. Tell her that you know the table is reserved and that you will be on your way shortly! If the reserving parties arrive, you must leave. If they don't come, then you can stay and order food if you like.

"Oans, zwoa, drei, Gsuffa"

No Oktoberfest is complete without this lively traditional song! Most beer tents feature traditional German bands, and every 20 minutes or so they break into a song called *Ein Prosit*. This is essential knowledge for the beer tents of Oktoberfest, so grab your beer, sway with your neighbors, and sing along!

> Ein Prosit Lyrics:
>
> Ein Prosit, Ein Prosit (Ayn Prawseet, Ayn Prawseet)
> Der Gemütlichkeit (Dare Gae-meet-lich-kite)
> Ein Prosit, Ein Prosit (Ayn Prawseet, Ayn Prawseet)
> Der Gemütlichkeit (Dare Gae-meet-lich-kite)

After the band plays this song, everyone raises their glasses and says: "Oans, zwoa, drei, Gsuffa!" meaning "one, two, three, drink!" You must sing this song and drink after each song. It's the law. *At least that is what they say*!

Zugspitze

Don't miss out on the Oktoberfest festivities on Germany's highest mountain! Take the gondola or the cog wheel train up to the summit and enjoy your fest beer at Germany's highest Biergarten or on Germany's highest mountain…you get the idea. You will be entertained with live music, spectacular views, and delicious food.

ALMTREIB
Until the cows come home…

September

In the springtime, farmers will lead their animals up into the higher meadows of the Alps. This is done to help make the animals more robust and healthier. In September, each village will celebrate the safe return of their cows or sheep with a street festival.

The lead cow (*Kranzkuh)* will be decorated with an elaborate wreath, followed by the rest of the herd. As long as there have been no deaths or injuries to the herd, they will be adorned with ornamental head-dresses and huge bells.

The best place to check on tentative dates is: http://www.bayern.by/almabtrieb-viehscheid-bayern.

ENG VALLEY
Autumn leaves and maple syrup in Austria

September

For bright and beautiful fall foliage, a trip to the alpine village of Eng should be on your list. With 600-year-old maple trees, this area in the Tyrolean Alps of the Karwendel has over 2000 maple trees. Cows graze the plentiful 590 hectares (just shy of 1500 acres). The fresh milk is processed on the mountain and available to purchase in the shops, as well as fresh yogurt, butter, and *Engalm* cheese.

The Almdorf *Engalm* (1227m) is a working farm and a step back in time, with its old wooden houses. There are several cottages surrounding the area, providing plenty of hiking choices.

Directions: You can reach the Eng valley by car from Garmisch, taking the B2 road (direction Mittenwald). Follow signs to Krun and Wallgau, continue until Vorderiss. You will take this toll road through the forest and cross into Austria. After crossing the bridge, make a right and follow signs to Eng. You will pay a small toll to enter the valley.

17

SINCE YOU INSIST

It would nearly impossible and unrealistic for someone visiting Garmisch-Partenkirchen not to visit the castles inspired by King Ludwig II. Since the purpose of this book is to encourage you to get off the beaten path and discover different ways to see Bavaria, I have chosen not to focus in any great detail about Neuschwanstein or Schloss Linderhof.

You should definitely see these castles if time permits. Each is a magical step back into time and into the mind of the Fairy Tale King. However, I would like to make some important recommendations that could make your visit more enjoyable.

Neuschwanstein:

Book your tickets online. If you wait until you arrive, you will most likely get a late afternoon ticket, sometimes hours after your arrival. http://www.hohenschwangau.de/ticketcenter.0.html.

Estimate an hour to arrive at the castle entrance for your tour. A horse carriage or shuttle bus is available if you prefer not to walk. The horses will trot up the original path to the castle and cost you €6 one way per person. The horse queue begins near the Hotel Müller. The shuttle bus queue begins just a bit further up the road and will cost €1 each way.

Download the Acoustic Bavaria: Neuschwanstein Castle app. This will give you everything you need to know about the castle, King Ludwig II's history, and so much more! acoustic-bavaria-neuschwanstein-castle.appstore.io

Return via the Pöllat Gorge, if open. Leaving the Marienbrücke and walking toward the castle, you will find a well-marked path to your right. This path will provide you with some great views of the bridge.

Directions: From Garmisch-Partenkirchen, drive toward Reutte on B23. You will cross the border in Griesen, continue on B23 until you reach the end of the road. Turn right toward Lermoos. Continue to follow B179, exit to Füssen – Neuschwanstein. Continue on B17 and follow signs to Schloss Neuschwanstein.

Linderhof:

If time is an issue during your visit and you can only see one castle, this is the one I would recommend! Schloss Linderhof is the only large castle where King Ludwig II actually lived; the castle has remained intact with all its original furnishings. Set amongst some very impressive terraced gardens and a complex grotto dedicated to the works of Wagner, these palace grounds will not disappoint.

Plan to spend a leisurely day, and allow plenty of time to explore the magnificent gardens. Tours are given frequently in different languages; advanced booking is not necessary.

If needed, wheelchairs are available at the cash desk, ask or call ahead to request one.

Note: at the time of this publication, the Venus Grotto will be closing for a renovation period of five years.

Directions: from Garmisch, travel on route B23 toward Munich. Turn left when you arrive in Oberau, following signs to Ettal, Oberammergau, and Murnau. Upon leaving Ettal, you will turn left onto ST2060. Follow signs to Schloss Linderhof.

18

TRAVELING WITHOUT THE CAR

In the case that you arrive to Garmisch-Partenkirchen without your own transportation, do not worry and do not let that stop you from exploring the area! Public transportation in Europe is awesome and with the right tools, you can easily find a plan to suit your needs.

My first recommendation is to seriously consider booking a private tour. Not only will you will get a personalized tour from someone who knows the area's history, but they can also provide transportation.

I highly recommend All Things Garmisch. www.allthingsgarmisch.com. This tour company is owned and operated by Jake Doherty, who has a vast knowledge of this area and will make your trip memorable.

Secondly, do some research online with the various transportation services. Many of them have mobile apps which can be helpful in finding the next bus or constructing your travel day.

- www.bahn.de: For train information and timetables
- https://meinfernbus.de/: An affordable local bus service with direct transportation to Munich, Seefeld, Innsbruck, Augsburg, and many more destinations.

Bayernpass

When traveling as a small group by train and subway, you need to buy the *Bayernpass.*

This ticket allows unlimited travel on all regional and suburban Deutche Bahn trains (no ICE trains) within the Bayern state. It is available for first and second-class travel. The cost is €23 for second class and €34.50 for first class. Five persons may travel together on the same ticket. Each additional person pays only €5. Children under 15 years travel for free when accompanied by a parent or grandparent.

This ticket also includes the following destinations: Salzburg, Kufstein, Reutte, and Ulm.

Travel on this ticket is valid weekdays from 09:00. – 03:00 the following day (18 hours). On Saturdays, Sundays, and public holidays, it is valid from midnight. – 03:00 the following day (27 hours).

Werdenfelspass

This pass covers a smaller area of travel and allows unlimited travel on all regional and suburban Deutche Bahn trains (no ICE trains) between Munich central train station and Tutzing, Kochel, Oberammergau and Mittenwald. Travel on this ticket has no time constraints.

The cost is €19 for second class and €27.50 for first class. Five persons may travel together on the same ticket. Each additional person pays only €4 for second class and €12.50 for first class. Up to three children from 6 -15 years old can travel for free.

19

RESTAURANTS

"Can you recommend a good place to eat?" is a question I hear often-- and I am happy to share my favorites! Thankfully, Garmisch has many great choices and it is not too touristy although some international fast food chains do have restaurants here.

Quick Bites

Hausberg Hütte: Yummy hot off the grill brats, the perfect snack or lunch while skiing. This hut is only open during the ski season. Location: Bottom of Hausberg Gondola.

Dönner: Originally from Turkey, this rotisserie meat is shaved off into fresh flat bread and garnished with salad and special sauces. There are several locations in Garmisch and each one is unique! Here are two possibilities:

Imbiß Bodrum: Von-Brug-Strasse 22 (by Müller and Hervis) features turkey meat and, in my opinion, is the best!

Ali Baba: Am Kurpark 17 (just off pedestrian street) serving tasty Turkish-Arabic food.

Vegetarian

Gasthaus zur Schranne: There are many restaurants featuring vegetarian options, but if you really want something special, make this your choice. Griessstrasse 4, Garmisch-Partenkirchen.

Mukkefuck: A cozy bistro café' featuring traditional and international cuisine. This is the place to come for salads (the dressing is amazing!) Zugspitzestrasse 3, Garmisch-Partenkirchen.

German specialties

Spatzenhäus'l: Truly the best schnitzel and haxen I have had! The schnitzels are huge, crispy and delicious. The Haxen (pork knuckle) is the right size and a perfect "crunch to edibility" ratio (my standard for a good haxen). Waxensteinstrasse 21, Grainau

Werdenfelser-Hof: Traditional Bavarian cuisine in a cozy wood paneled restaurant with young boys who perform the *Schuhplattler* dance while you enjoy your dinner. They proudly serve Munich's oldest brewery beer, Augustiner. Ludwigstrasse 58, Garmisch-Partenkirchen.

Maronis: Excellent choice for schnitzels! Morehnplatz 10, Garmisch-Partenkirchen.

Special Occasion

Hammersbacher Hütte: A small, cozy cottage located next to the Hammersbach stream. Kreuzeckweg 4, Grainau.

Schmölzer Wirt: Beautiful Tyrolian decor and a menu featuring classic German dishes, with an elevated touch. *Be sure to see the canvas prints on the way to the restrooms – historic photos of workers in the Partnachklamm. Griesener Strasse 7, Grainau.

Kaiserschmarnn

Toni Bartl's Kaiserschmarnn Alm: This charming cabin just above the Graseck gondola has the best Kaiserschmarnn I've ever tried! This delicious and pleasant caramelized crepe is cut into strips and served with a generous sprinkling of sugar.

It is said that *Kaiserschmarnn* (Emperor's Mess) was the favored dish of the Austrian Emperor, Franz Joseph I. Supposedly, when serving this dessert to his Emperor, the servant tripped and quickly tossed all the pieces onto the plate. It was a success and the Emperor loved it.

Location: Olympic ski stadium. Follow the pedestrian path towards the Partnachklamm. Take the Graseck gondola (GraseckBahn), follow the path around the Hotel Graseck, turn right and continue for 15 minutes to Toni Bartl's.

Estimated time: 20-30 minutes on foot, and after arriving with the gondola 15 minutes more on foot.

ACKLNOWLEDGEMENTS

This book would not have been possible without the support of my family, who encouraged me to continue exploring, planning, and dreaming.

Thank you to my Mother, who taught me the love of travel. To my daughter, Erika, who always challenged me to do more. To my daughter, Maria, who supported me by joining me on many of these trips!

Most importantly, to my husband Rick, for you unfaltering support, encouragement and "eagle eye" for detail. I love you. Thank you for not letting me give up!

To my sister, Liza and her family who tested out many of these adventures and helped in the design cover.

A heartfelt thank you to my colleagues and friends from Garmisch Outdoor Recreation: Jessica Roberson, Drew Benson, Tom Sheaffer, Tom Creley, Paul Dutro, and Kelly Joines, for your encouragement to explore Garmisch-Partenkirchen and share it with others.

A hug of gratitude to my friends who took the time to review, edit and help make this book better: Jeanine Rolfe Ritzel and Kelly Joines.

A special thank you to Jean Callaghan for all her editorial work, it was incredible.

DISCLAIMER

The author takes no responsibility for any information in this book. Trails and terrain conditions can always change, so local and up-to-date knowledge should always be consulted when venturing into the local mountains. No matter the activity, especially outdoor physical activity, readers should take the appropriate precautions by consulting the appropriate outdoor safety recommendations, for any time of year. Of note is that weather patterns, particularly in the mountains, can change rather quickly and drastically, so outdoor enthusiasts should always prepare for worst case scenarios. Here are a few informative sources:

http://exotichikes.com/11-ways-to-stay-safe-while-hiking-what-every-hiker-should-know/

http://www.americanhiking.org/gear-resources/tips-for-your-next-hike/

http://www.hikingbeginner.com/Hiking_Safety_Tips.html

https://www.alpenverein.de/

REFERENCES

"200 Years of German Beer | European Traveler." 200 Years of German Beer | European Traveler. http://www.europeantraveler.net/attractions-germanbeer.php.

@TriciaAMitchell. "A Valley ablaze: The König-Ludwig-Feuer in Oberammergau, Germany." Travels with Tricia A Mitchell. 2015. Accessed January 18, 2016. https://triciaannemitchell.com/2015/08/16/koenig-ludwig-feuer-oberammergau-king-ludwig-bonfire/.

Amend, Rita. "Oktoberfest Munich 2016 – Facts, Events, History." GermanyInsiderFacts. http://www.germany-insider-facts.com/oktoberfest-munich.html#.VaC5M_mqqko.

The Atlantic. http://www.theatlantic.com/international/archive/2015/04/how-the-beer-garden-came-to-be/391343/.

Barrow, Mandy. "The Legend of Saint George and the Dragon." Project Britain British Life and Culture. Accessed September 11, 2016. https://projectbritan.com/stgeorge2.html.

Beer_jar_128. [Digital image]. (n.d.) Retrieved from www.flaticon.com.

Brauner, Horst. "Französischer Markt in Oberursel." Termine. http://www.le-marche-francais.de/termine/.

"Cross-country Skiing | Ammergauer Alps." Ammergauer Alps. http://www.ammergauer-alpen.de/en/Winter-vacation/Cross-country-skiing

"Corpus Christi in Germany." http://www.timeanddate.com/holidays/germany/corpus-christi.

(DAV), Deutscher Alpenverein E.V. "Geschichte Des DAV." Deutscher Alpenverein (DAV). http://www.alpenverein.de/der-dav/geschichte-des-dav_aid_12067.html.

"Ein Prosit Song Lyrics." Oktoberfest Tours.

http://www.oktoberfesttours.travel/ein-prosit-song-lyrics/.

Exclamation_in_a_circle_sketch. [Digital image]. (n.d.) Retrieved from www.flaticon.com.

Fork. [Digital image]. (n.d.) Retrieved from www.flaticon.com.

"Fronleichnam: Was Katholiken Feiern - Und wo Feiertag Ist." Http://www.hna.de. 2016. http://hna.de/welt/fronleichnam-bedeutung-des-katholischen-festes-in-einigen-bundeslaendern-2016-feiertag-zr-6429121.html.

"Fusswallfahrten: Geh-bete." Pilgrim Ways. http://wies-kirche.de/pilgrim-ways.en.html

GmbH, BAYERN TOURISMUS Marketing. "Bavaria Southern Germany - Christmas Markets Oberammergau." BAYERN TOURISMUS Marketing GmbH. http://www.bavaria.by/christmas-market-in-oberammergau-germany.

Https://www.facebook.com/tonlinede. "Nicht überall Gesetzlicher Feiertag: Fronleichnam 2016: Darum Feiern Wir Dieses Katholische Hochfest. "Www.t-online.de.2016. http://www.t-online.de/nachrichten/id_74249268/fronleichnam-2016-das-steckt-hinter-dem-katholischen-feiertag.html.

"Karneval, Fastnacht Und Fasching in Garmisch-Partenkirchen." Karneval, Fastnacht Und Fasching in Garmisch-Partenkirchen. http://cities.eurip.com/stadt/garmisch-partenkirchen/fasching/.

"Kolbensattel Lodge." Kolbensattel Lodge. http://kolbensattel.de/en/kolbensattel-lodge.

Landeshauptstadt München, Redaktion Munich, State Capital, Editorial Team. "The Munich Christmas Market – a unique Experience." Landeshauptstadt München. http://www.muenchen.de/rathaus/home_en/Tourist-Office/Events/Christmas/Erlebnis_e.

"The Legend of Saint George." Saint George (Golden Legend). Accessed September 10, 2016. http://pitt.edu/-dash/stgeorge1.html.

"Loewenbraeu.de." Loewenbraeu.de. http://www.loewenbraeu.de/.

"Mandarin-Orange - Vignette Color 2016." Toll Sticker. Munich Events. http://www.worldtravelguide.net/munich/events.

Muenchen.de. "History of the Oktoberfest." Muenchen.de. http://www.muenchen.de/int/en/events/oktoberfest/history.html.

Muenchen.de. "Spargelsaison Und Spargelanstisch." Muenchen.de. http://www.muenchen.de/leben/typisch-muenchen/spargel.html.

"Partnachklamm." Partnachklamm. Accessed August 06, 2016. http://www.partnachklamm.eu/.

Price_tag_with_mountains_128. [Digital image]. (n.d.) Retrieved from www.flaticon.com.

Restaurant_cutlery_circular_symbol_of_a_spoon_and_a_fork_in_a_circle_128. [Digital image]. (n.d.) Retrieved from www.flaticon.com.

"Safety and an unforgettable experience – 10 tips on safe and healthy hiking." Gapa.de. http://www.gapa.de/blobs/2_1_1_1_tipps_zum_wandern_en.pdf.

Sausage_on_a_fork_128. [Digital image]. (n.d.) Retrieved from www.flaticon.com.

Smith, Gavin. D. *Beer: A Global History.*

"Spanfankerl Pass – Die Krampusse Und Perchten Aus München." Sparifankerl Pass – Die Krampusse Und Perchten Aus München. http://www.sparifankerl-pass.de/index.php?article_id=59.

"Steckenberg Erlebnisberg in Unterammergau. Sommerrodelbahn und Skigebiet Im Ammertal." Steckenberg
Erlebnisberg in Unterammergau. Sommerrodelbahn Und Skigebiet Im Ammertal. http://www.steckenberg.de/

"Tollwood Winterfestival 2016." Tollwood München: Veranstaltungen, Konzerte, Theater, Weihnachtsmarkt. http://www.tollwood.de/winterfestival-2016/.

User, Super. "Über Uns." Über Uns. Accessed 10 October, 2015. http://www.bayernhaus-garmisch.de/.

Wikipedia contributors. "Zugspitze." *Wikipedia, The Free Encyclopedia,* https://en.wikipedia.org/windex.php?toitel=Zugspitze&oldid=738656251

(accessed September 13, 2016.

"WELCOME TO THE HOME OF SPATEN BEER." Spaten München. http://www.spatenbeer.com/.

About the author

Susan Steinke is a California native who loves traveling and possesses a sense of adventure.

Through her husband's U.S. military and subsequent federal service, she has embraced the Army lifestyle as a spouse, enjoying and learning as much as possible about her new environment. She has lived in California, Oregon, Indiana, Virginia, Massachusetts, Missouri, and Oklahoma. She has traveled Europe extensively with her family while living in Italy, France and Germany.

Her desire to share her lessons inspired her to write this book. She continues to explore Italy, Spain, Austria...and beyond!

Follow Susan:
Facebook @SusanCSteinke
Instagram @Garmisch_hiddengems

CPSIA information can be obtained
at www.ICGtesting.com
Printed in the USA
BVHW061158130220
572293BV00008B/338